Organization Development and Society

Organization Development and Society: Theory and Practice of Organization Development Consulting offers a new approach for the practice of organization development (OD). The new approach, a habitus-oriented OD (HOOD), sees consultees' thinking and behavior a result of habitus, a cognitive structure developed historically in endless interactions between human behavior and social structures. HOOD has two goals:

The first goal is to redefine the objectives of individually oriented OD. The focus on habitus and social structure allows individually oriented OD scholars and practitioners to keep their subjective approach, which searches for consultees' inner world. However, this subjectivity searches not only for consultees' psychological but their social dispositions. It views the individual level, the habitus, as a site of social dispositions that from within the individual consultees generate thoughts and behaviors in a way that closely corresponds with the organization's social structure; with power relations and social positions and with accepted metaphors and common language. The HOOD links the concept of habitus to the field of OD and in so doing provides an alternative way to incorporate the individual and the social in OD.

HOOD's second goal is to re/position OD between organizations and society and thus to produce a consulting practice that is both pragmatic and human. It is pragmatic since incorporation of habitus enables the consultant to liberate consultees' perspectives and behavior from the organization's social and structural hoops and to use these perspectives in processes of change and development. Considering the habitus as central to consulting projects is human since it enables consultants (and consultees) to identify the responsibility for organizational problems (and other phenomena) not only at the level of the individual but also at the level of the organization and the environment outside the organization.

Baruch Shimoni is the founder and head of the Graduate Program in Organization Development at Bar-Ilan University Israel.

Routledge Studies in Organizational
Change & Development
Series Editor
Bernard Burnes

Rethinking Organizational Change
The Role of Dialogue, Dialectic & Polyphony in the Organization
Muayyad Jabri

Organizational Change and Temporality
Bending the Arrow of Time
Patrick Dawson and Christopher Sykes

Reconsidering Change Management
Applying Evidence-Based Insights in Change Management Practice
*Steven ten Have, Wouter ten Have, Anne-Bregje Huijsmans,
and Maarten Otto*

Rethinking Culture
Embodied Cognition and the Origin of Culture in Organizations
David G. White, Jr

Academic Practitioner Research Partnerships
Developments, Complexities and Opportunities
Edited by Jean Bartunek and Jane McKenzie

The Social Psychology of Change Management
Theories and an Evidence-Based Perspective on Social
and Organizational Beings
*Steven ten Have, John Rijsman, Wouter ten Have
and Joris Westhof*

Organization Development and Society
Theory and Practice of Organization Development Consulting
Baruch Shimoni

For a full list of titles in this series, please visit www.routledge.com

Organization Development and Society

Theory and Practice of Organization Development Consulting

Baruch Shimoni

Routledge
Taylor & Francis Group

NEW YORK AND LONDON

First published 2019
by Routledge
605 Third Avenue, New York, NY 10017

and by Routledge
2 Park Square, Milton Park, Abingdon, Oxon, OX14 4RN

First issued in paperback 2021

Routledge is an imprint of the Taylor & Francis Group, an informa business

Library of Congress Cataloging-in-Publication Data
Names: Shimoni, Baruch, author.
Title: Organization development and society : theory and practice of organization development consulting / Baruch Shimoni.
Description: New York : Routledge, 2019. | Series: Routledge studies in organizational change & development | Includes index.
Identifiers: LCCN 2018059784 | ISBN 9781138569645 (hardback) | ISBN 9781351264846 (ebook)
Subjects: LCSH: Organizational change. | Business consultants.
Classification: LCC HD58.8 .S495 2019 | DDC 001—dc23
LC record available at https://lccn.loc.gov/2018059784

ISBN 13: 978-0-367-78670-0 (pbk)
ISBN 13: 978-1-138-56964-5 (hbk)

Typeset in Sabon
by Apex CoVantage, LLC

To Omri, with all a father's love

Contents

Tables

Acknowledgments

I thank my students and consultees for giving me the opportunity to develop the ideas presented in this book. Their helpful comments and insights made the book infinitely better. I thank the participants in the International Conference on Business and Internet, held in Taipei and Hiroshima in the summers of 2016–2018, for their sensitive comments and help in the process of developing the book's ideas. Great thanks to the participants in the conference of Knowledge, Culture and Change in Organization held in British Columbia University in the summer of 2013, where I first presented the book's ideas. Special thanks to Harriet Bergmann for her advice and comments through all the stages of this book and to Eyal Ben-Ari of the Hebrew University for his careful reading and significant suggestions. Finally, I would like to offer my deep appreciation to the anonymous readers of the book's proposal and to Prof. Bernard Burnes, the editor of Routledge Studies in Organizational Change & Development for their comments, suggestions and editing.

1 Introduction

The Book's Argument

Like many other OD scholars and practitioners with an individualistic orientation, in my OD consulting career I used to think and work largely with therapeutic discourse and practices. Specifically, I focused the change process on consultees' psychological dispositions, their self-development and personal growth (Schein, 1969a, 1987a; Voronov and Woodworth, 2012).

Many writers have proposed definitions for OD (for more definitions see Church, Waclawski, and Seigel, 1996; French and Bell, 1999; Lippitt and Lippitt, 1978). Although the definitions differ in details, Paul Lawrence and Jay Lorsch's (1969, p. 9) definition represents some common characteristics:

> OD is an effort (1) *planned*, (2) *organization-wide*, and (3) *managed from the top*, to (4) increase *organization effectiveness* and *health* through (5) *planned interventions* in the organization's "process," using *behavioral-science* knowledge.

Writers define OD, then, as a planned change practice managed from the top and focused on the organization as one whole (macro level, subparts and individuals) to increase effectiveness.

OD is also defined as a helping profession (Lippitt and Lippitt, 1978; Ottaway, 1983; Schein, 1999, 2009). As in other helping professions such as psychology, social work and clinical sociology, OD consultants build helping relationships with consultees (individuals and groups) in which they encourage consultees to take responsibility for the organization's problems and develop concepts and practices to diagnose and find solutions for these problems.[1] OD consultants do not work *for* but *with* consultees to help them help themselves and their organizations.

Today, after 25 years of research, consulting and teaching using concepts from the sociology of organizations, specifically Critical Management Studies (CMS) and the sociology of Pierre Bourdieu, I understand that the therapeutic perspective that dominated my work was wrong. That is, I have learned that using intensive therapeutic discourse and practices in order to directly change consultees' psychological dispositions, and hence their thinking and behavior, does not change organizations (Beer, Eisenstat, and Spector, 1990; Bradford and Porras, 2005; Fincham and Clark, 2002). I realized that consultees' poor performance, for example, does not always reflect psychological dispositions such as low commitment and lack of responsibility, and that those dispositions were what I wanted to help organizations to change.[2]

Often, the therapeutic discourse (e.g., "what do you feel about the change process?") and practices (e.g., group workshops that encourage participants to take direct responsibility for the organization's poor performance) helped consultees through the change process. It created satisfaction and a feeling of accomplishment. However, focusing consulting processes on consultees' psychological dispositions, as I have learned in my own experience, created a common understanding that the individual self is a highly important resource that I should constantly cultivate (Costea, Crump, and Amiridis, 2008). This understanding and thus my unceasing efforts to work on a consultee's self, distracted our (my consultees' and my own) attention from seriously searching for the source of problems in structures on the level of the organization such as unequal allocation of resources, unclear vision and goals and poor management. Furthermore, it distracted *my* attention from questioning the existing power structure and power relations and thus from the fact that I was taking an overly management-oriented approach focused on fitting a consultee's self to expectations and goals defined by those who invited me, usually management (Boje, 2012).

Following OD's traditional goals and like many other writers (Bradford and Porras, 2005; Greiner and Cummings, 2005; Katz and Kahn, 1966; Lawrence and Lorsch, 1969; Voronov and Woodworth, 2012) who hold systemic orientation and emphasize technology, culture and social structure (common language, organizing metaphors, power relations), I no longer focus solely on consultees' psychological dispositions. My reluctance to focus solely on consultees' personal development and growth and on their psychological intentions and motivations allows me to concentrate just as much on the role of the organization's social structure in producing their thoughts and behaviors.

The understanding that in my consulting work I am interested not only in an individual's self but also in social structures encouraged me to write a book on individually oriented OD from a sociological perspective, yet one question remained. Can we separate the personal from the social? Is "resistance to change", a common behavior in organizational change processes, for example, a personal or a social phenomenon? Is it a psychological or a sociological occurrence? Those who see resistance to change as a psychological phenomenon believe that it is a defense mechanism or that it represents other psychological dispositions such as frustration, anxiety, fear and aggression (Schein, 1987b). Those who see resistance to change as a social phenomenon view it as an expression of structures such as unequal division of labor, asymmetric power relations and poor management (Ford, Ford, and D'Amelio, 2008).

I claim, however, that these two perspectives (the personal and the social) are problematic since they miss the opportunity to understand the other's reciprocal influences. Understanding resistance to change, or any other behavior in organizations, I claim, entails adopting both perspectives, the personal and the social, and searching for the dialectic relations between the two. Specifically, following Pierre Bourdieu's (1989) theory of practice, which questions equally the personal and the social (personal practice and social structures) and the role of the dialectic relations between the two in generating individual and group thoughts and behaviors, the approach presented in this book understands resistance as a practice produced by social dispositions, or habitus (Shimoni, 2017). Habitus is a cognitive construct produced in dialectic relations between personal practice and social structures and thus represents not the personal or the social roots of resistance but the *combined* roots of the two (Bourdieu, 1989).

A First Glance on the Concept of Habitus

Habitus consists of a set of durable social dispositions such as worldview, schema of thinking and practical knowledge (Bourdieu, 1989). Social agents (individuals or groups) adopt these social dispositions from the social structures of their family, gender group, ethnic group and working organization through a process of socialization. Social structures consist of common language, organizing metaphors, power relations and control over symbolic and physical resources. Once internalized by social agents, these social structures are taken for granted, an inner structure, natural and durable dispositions—a structured structure embedded in the social agent (Bourdieu, 1989).

Although habitus is structured and embedded in the social agent, it does not respond mechanically to the social structure. It literally becomes part of the social agent's body, his or her thoughts, emotions and physical-bodily dispositions, what Bourdieu calls the *hexis* (Bourdieu, 1977). Habitus thus functions also as a "structuring structure" (Bourdieu, 1989, p. 18) that shapes people's current and upcoming practices (Maton, 2014). Like culture, habitus infuses social reality (Foster, 1986). It is "what the social world leaves in each and every one of us in our proneness to act and react in a certain manner, likes and dislikes, ways of perceiving, thinking and feeling" (Lahire, 2002, p. 596). It exists in the form of mental and "corporeal schemata, a matrix of perception, appreciation, and action" (Bourdieu and Wacquant, 1992, pp. 16–18) that from within the social agent *predisposes* the way he or she develops new and creative thoughts and behaviors (Bourdieu, 1989, 1990).

Habitus, however, always relates to power relations determined mainly by the "capital" social agents have (Bourdieu, 1989). Among types of capital are "economic capital" (control of tangible resources such as machines, commodities and financial budgets), "human capital" (knowledge, skills and expertise), "symbolic capital" (prestige and reputation), "social capital" (the ability to use capital of other social agents to promote one's own interests) and "cultural capital" (arbitrary attributions like accepted language) (Everett, 2002). For example, managers and other dominant agents in organizations have cultural capital derived from their competencies (language, significant knowledge and techniques) to run organizations. They also have symbolic capital, prestige, for being the leaders of the organization, and most often, they have social capital, derived from the use of other participants' capital to advance their own particular interests.

For Bourdieu, then, the habitus is not a constant and neutral but a dynamic and constructed entity that continually changes in accordance with power and social positions derived from control over symbolic and material capitals (Battilana, 2006; Everett, 2002; Özbilgin and Ahu Tatli, 2005; Wacquant, 1989). As a cognitive structure, the habitus is a mirror image of symbolic and material capital and thus it overcomes the subjective-objective dichotomy in explaining thoughts and behaviors.

It is also important to remember that habitus is a product of a specific social field in which people play a game with defined rules (Kerr and Robinson, 2009). Rules include taken-for-granted social regulations such as ways of thinking, power relations and distribution of capital. The field's rules of the game shape social agents' thinking and behavior—they allow and restrict behavior. Thus, understanding the way social agents think and behave entails a search for the field's unquestioned rules and structures of power in which their habitus has been produced and developed (Bourdieu, 1989, p. 327). Habitus is the internalization of rules belonging to a specific social field.

Considering the role of social fields in shaping individuals' and groups' behavior takes this book back to OD's origins—to the 1940s–1960s, the time before OD was almost totally engaged by therapeutic psychological discourse and practices (Bradford and Porras, 2005). It goes back to Kurt Lewin (1939), OD's founding father, and to his "Field Theory" that, like Bourdieu (who followed Lewin, while both followed Cassirer; see Vandenberghe, 1999, p. 52) seeks to create a bridge between the personal and the social (Friedman, 2011; Lapidot-Lefler et al, 2015). The roots of field theory, say Bernard Burnes and David Bargal (2017, p. 93), are in both physics and psychology, specifically in the Gestalt school of psychology, according to which "behavior needs to be evaluated in the right context, taking into account the forces that affect it". In Lewin's words (1939, p. 868),

> To explain social behavior it is necessary to represent the structure of the total situation and the distribution of the forces in it.

Although both Lewin and Bourdieu assume that it is impossible to understand behavior without considering the social field, there are at least two significant differences between their understanding of the relations between the personal and the social. First, Lewin sees the social field as a *shared* "total-situation" that gives meaning to behavior. Bourdieu, in contrast, views the social field as an *arena of competition and struggles* over all sorts of forms of capital in which, says David Swartz (1997, p. 63), "competitive distinction, domination, and misperception" prevail over sharing and cooperation. Second, Lewin sees the social field's structure and the social agent's behavior (the social and the personal) as two interacting but *separate* entities in which the social field inspires behavior. Bourdieu, on the other hand, sees the social field's structure and the social agent's behavior as *one entity* enacted in habitus.

Viewing structure and behavior as one entity embedded in habitus, HOOD assumes the individual consultee to be not a psychological subject, a passive agent who needs to be adapted to the outside social and cultural environment, as the individually oriented OD often sees him or her. Instead, HOOD assumes the individual consultee to be a sociological subject, an active agent who is an unseparated part of the array of structural opportunities and constraints within which his or her habitus is developed, positioned and operates. Understanding the individual consultee as a social subject, in my consulting experience served my consultees and me as a point of departure for changing the organization's social structures and the working conditions these structures create.

The Book's Goals

Bourdieu's (1989) theory of practice and especially the concept of habitus serve in this book as a point of departure in the development of a theoretical and practical approach for OD—a *habitus-oriented* OD (HOOD). The HOOD has two goals. The first goal is to redefine the objectives of individually oriented OD. Individually oriented OD focuses mainly on consultees' *psychological* dispositions; in contrast, HOOD focuses on consultees' *social* dispositions, or habitus. This focus on habitus, which is a cognitive construct of the social structure, allows individually oriented OD scholars and practitioners to keep their subjective approach, which searches for consultees' inner world. However, this subjectivity searches not only for consultees' psychological but their social dispositions. That is, it views the individual level, the habitus, as a site of cognitive social dispositions that from within the individual consultees generates thoughts and behaviors in a way that closely corresponds with the organization's social structure (Bourdieu, 1989), with power relations and social positions and with accepted metaphors and common language. The HOOD links the Bourdieuan concept of habitus to the field of OD and in so doing provides an alternative way to incorporate the individual and the social in OD.

By putting habitus, that embodies both behavior and structure, at the center of the consulting process, HOOD achieves its second goal: to re/root, or combine with OD's democratic and humanistic values and re/position it (OD) in between organizations and society and thus to produce a consulting practice that is both pragmatic and human. It is *pragmatic* since incorporation of habitus enables the practitioner to liberate consultees' perspectives and behavior from the organization's social and structural hoops and to use these perspectives in processes of change and development. In the book, I give examples of the development of consultees' "reflexivity" to habitus and to social structure. Bourdieu uses the term reflexivity to define "the activity of the social analyst who sets out to offer accounts of the practice of others" (Wacquant, 1989, pp. 26–27. Quoted by Deer, 2008, p. 195). By developing consultees' reflexivity to habitus and to social structure, I helped consultees liberate their behavior from the organizations' dominant structures (such as unequal power relations and asymmetric distribution of resources) and thus enabled them to create the kind of change based on wider and deeper knowledge.

Considering the habitus as central to consulting projects is *human* since it enables consultants (and consultees) to identify the responsibility for organizational problems (and other phenomena) not only at the level of the individual but also at the level of the organization and the environment outside the organization. As my examples show, in my consulting experience I found that a focus on habitus and social structure encouraged the people who invited me to the organization, usually powerful agents who lead the organization, to stop blaming non-managerial employees for causing organizational problems. Often, as we will see, the roots of these problems are found in structural elements such as social marginalization and problematic role definitions that those agents themselves created. A focus on habitus helps us solve these problems by working on individuals' social dispositions and the organization's structures.

The Habitus-Oriented OD (HOOD) as a Helping Profession

Almost 50 years ago, Chris Argyris (1972, p. 98) challenged sociology and sociologists (Peter Blau, James Thompson, Charley Perrow and John Goldthorpe) for focusing mainly on research and theory development while leaving practice outside their scope. What "model of intervention" do they have, he asked. "Would they work at the interpersonal level? . . . would they utilize group dynamics? If so, what theories of interpersonal and group dynamics would they utilize? How would these theories of change be integrated with their present theories?" Argyris continues by saying that sociologists should think in not only terms of theory development and giving feedback (to clients such as organizations' and union leaders) regarding their research findings. They should also develop ways to help clients use the knowledge sociologists have.

Sociology suggests answers to Argyris' questions in what it calls "Clinical Sociology" (Bruhn and Rebach, 2007, 2012). Like OD, Clinical Sociology offers a systematic framework for intervention in working organizations and in the community. Like OD consultants, clinical sociologists attempt to make changes in social arrangements and behavior. Intervention, for Clinical Sociology, is a dynamic process of cooperation between practicing sociologists and participants from within the organization.

Although Clinical Sociology provides valuable tools for developing and changing organizations and communities, which Argyris has noted as lacking in sociologists' work, in this book I remain within OD's boundaries. I write the book from within the OD field and use its ideas and practices for the development of HOOD.

Perhaps the most important idea HOOD adopts from individually oriented OD is the philosophy of helping. According to the philosophy of helping consultants help consultees (individuals and groups) to help themselves (Schein, 2009). The assumption here is that since consulting projects in organizations, in human systems, usually take place in face-to-face conversations, OD consultants need to acquire therapeutic practices. As Edgar Schein (2005) says, practices such as active listening, reflection and feedback enable consultants to establish helping relationships with consultees. Helping relationships are *trustful* relationships that allow OD consultants to get both the needed information on the organization and consultees' commitment to take responsibility for the change process (Lippitt and Lippitt, 1978; Zand, 2010). Following Graham Benjamin and Christopher Mabey (1993, p. 181; quoted by Burnes, 2012b, p. 140), then, the HOOD assumes that "while the primary stimulus for change remains those forces in the external environment, the primary motivator for how change is accomplished reside with the people within the organization".

HOOD's Dual Perspective

HOOD encourages OD consultants to adopt a dual perspective. The conceptual and practical origins of this perspective are in both the therapeutic psychology that frames OD's helping philosophy (Schein, 2009) and Pierre Bourdieu's theory of action (Bourdieu, 1989). The helping philosophy grants HOOD consultants the discourse and practices needed to create effective relationships with consultees and develop consultees' responsibility for the organizational change process. Bourdieu's theory of action grants HOOD consultants the ability to develop consultees reflexivity to habitus and thus to the organization's social structure and to their position in this structure.

HOOD, then, takes part in both psychological and sociological education. It encourages OD consultants to help consultees develop their responsibility for the change process and reflexivity to their (and others') habitus, hence to the organization's social structure and to positions in this structure.

Wedding of Organization Development (OD) and Critical Management Studies (CMS)

In this book, I integrate Bourdieu's theory of action, with its critical perspective, into the field of OD. Bourdieu's theory, which focuses on unquestioned structures of power, grants OD a theoretical and practical perspective to work on the organization's unseen processes of coercion and domination that marginalize, often oppress and even exclude non-managerial perspectives (Reynolds and Vince, 2004). According to Frank Dobbin (2008, p. 62), Bourdieu's theory of action offers "substantive insights about how modern systems of domination operate . . . revealing how power was embedded in everyday social relations and in individual consciousness".

Specifically, Bourdieu's theory of action helps HOOD to see that practices, especially of those in power who significantly control the organization's capital and high positions, are not neutral (Sieweke, 2014). Often, these practices represent management's genuine intentions to achieve the organization's goals. However, in other times and very often implicitly, these practices serve the immediate interests and goals of management and other influential groups in the organization. Put in simple terms, in this book I use Bourdieu's theory of action to offer a consulting approach, HOOD, that seeks to help organizations be "less controlling, less exploiting, less dominating, and more just" (Nathan and Whatley, 2006, pp. 65–66).

Offering a consulting approach that encourages less domination and more justice is not political. I do not aim to replace the individually oriented OD but to emancipate our view from its overly individualistic perspective by offering a new way to integrate the social with the individual through the concept of habitus. Bourdieu, as Michael Grenfell (2010, p. 88) points out, believed that everything is fundamentally political. However, he did not seek only political emancipation. Emancipation for Bourdieu is "from thinking and seeing the world in a certain way". It represents a call for reflexivity (Leander, 2001).

Researchers, say Bourdieu (Bourdieu and Wacquant, 1992, p. 183), simply become the "toys of social forces". For him the definition of a research object and the representation of its needs, perspectives and interests "entails a break with common sense [and from] representations shared by all" (Bourdieu and Wacquant, 1992, p. 235–237). "It involves", as Jeffery Everett (2002, p. 74) understands Bourdieu, "a radical doubting and necessitates a critical discussion". To avoid becoming toys of social forces, Bourdieu encourages researchers to "turn the instruments of science on themselves" (Bourdieu and Wacquant, 1992, pp. 36–214), exactly as he does in his criticism of the field of higher education (Bourdieu, 1988). Bourdieu calls on social scientists to reflect on their own research field and search for the ways in which knowledge and theory shape their claims.

Scholars of management and organization studies, as Jost Sieweke (2014, p. 9) shows, do reflect on their academic field. For example, they research fashions in organizational theory (Bort and Kieser, 2011), circulation of ideas (Battilana, Anteby, and Sengul, 2010), "differences between the European and North American management and organization studies" (Meyer and Boxenbaum, 2010) and the non-natural role of business planning that embodies hidden curriculum and activities that undermine participants' own capital (Oakes, Townley, and Cooper, 1998). This is how scholars of organizational studies should understand Bourdieu's reflexivity, according to Mustafa Özbilgin, Abu Tatli, and Mary Queen (2005, p. 859),

> [R]eflexivity for Bourdieu does not simply refer to endless "autobiographical referentiality," or to the unconscious dispositions of the individual researcher, but to an examination of the "epistemological unconscious" and the "social organization" of the discipline . . . Hence, the viewpoint of a scholar of organizational studies is a particular perspective that is not simply the expression of an individual viewpoint but an analytic disposition that is part of and formed in and by the "collective unconscious"—habitus—of an academic field.

I believe that Özbilgin, Tatli and Queen's expectation that scholars of management and organizations studies adopt Bourdieu's reflexivity is extremely relevant to OD scholars and practitioners. In their research and practice, they (OD scholars and practitioners) should uncover the "epistemological unconscious" and the "social organization" of the OD field and explicitly relate to its analytic dispositions that are part of and formed by this "collective unconscious"—the habitus of the OD as a social field. As Laura Bierema (2010, p. 34) correctly claims, OD scholars and practitioners should "take a more critical approach to OD by reflecting on actions and questioning assumptions, particularly those that are taken-for-granted, and privilege certain groups over others".

Specifically, there is a need to adopt a critical perspective that, as Joshua Nathan and Art Whatley (2006, p. 67) say, "mobilizes the powers of critical reasoning to uncover and scrutinize the underlying assumptions associated with O.D".

Critical reflections, however, are not new to OD writers. Examples are the works of Maxim Voronov (2005, 2008) who offers collaboration between CMS and OD that both, as he rightly claims, hold a humanistic philosophy attempting to liberate people from restricting structures. The work of Bierema (2010) develops a critical OD practice that aims to challenge the "status quo and replace it with more democratic and equitable practices, politics and structures" (p. 27). Other OD writers reflect on OD's "overly individual orientation" or "psychologism" (Voronov and Woodworth, 2012), managerialist perspective (Boje, 2012) and limited care for the organization as a whole (Bradford and Porras, 2005). Similarly, in her research into the many areas that critical OD should focus on, Nicoll (1999, quoted by Nathan and Whatley, 2006, pp. 64–65) encourages OD scholars and practitioners to reflect on the "kinds of dark things [that] are going on inside our client systems" (p. 5). Those dark things are (p. 6):

• Exploiting (. . .) segments of the workforce.
• Forcing employees into maladaptive personal responses.
• Disenfranchising almost everyone.
• Doing a greater proportion of damage to the environment.
• Destroying or homogenizing whole cultures.
• Knowingly selling harmful products and violating human rights; and
• Undermining democracies and democratic processes.

Searching for social structure and power relations and thus for a more humane and pragmatic consulting practice, HOOD meets many of those critical goals and expectations. Yet, most of the writers discussed (but Bierema, 2010) do not integrate their critical reflections into *strategic* OD, as I do in this book. As a scholar-practitioner, positioned in the academic and in the practical fields, dedicated both to critical and to strategic perspectives, I use Bourdieu's theory of action not to offer theoretical and critical reflections per se. Reflection is not the end-point but a starting point of my intellectual project that aims to develop a *critical OD practice*. This practice, HOOD, offers not only "alternative models and theories", as Andrew Van de Ven and Paul Johnson (2006, p. 815) claim in their research into the production of knowledge in the existing gap between theory and practice, but a new "actionable scientific knowledge" (Tenkasi and Hai, 2008, p. 54).

The HOOD, which focuses mainly on increasing consultees' reflexivity to habitus and to social structure, thus has the potential to help consultants end practices of domination and foster democratic and egalitarian practices that promote more independent and autonomic consultees (Alvesson and Willmott, 1996, p. 17). Specifically, in an era of rapid change and high competition that pushes managements in modern organizations to struggle hard for fast profitability, the focus on habitus allows OD to keep its core values aiming to achieve economic goals while freeing employees from limiting structures (Burnes, 2012a). It allows OD scholars and practitioners to consider not only the reciprocal relations between profit and capitalist management-oriented practices but also the interests and possible impact on all the organization's stakeholders.

The critical perspective, then, positions the HOOD in OD's original role as a bridge between organizations and society, in a place that is people *and* task oriented, a place that considers equally the human and the pragmatic, individuals and effectiveness, social needs and profitability, society and organizations. It represents OD's traditional attempts to

> [H]elp organizations contribute to society while providing meaningful, creative opportunities for work and growth without destroying organizations . . . [this social order, also] resists and redirects the drive to either extreme—organizational exploitation of man and man's exploitation of organizations.
>
> (Zand, 2010, p. 424)

Who Are the Readers of the Book?

The book has a diverse target readership. First are the scholar-practitioners who articulate OD's theoretical and practical discourse in academic articles and books. The second group is OD instructors and consultants who teach and conduct OD. Third are the instructors, students and consultants in therapeutic fields such as psychology and social work who can apply the book's sociological perspective that views personal, organizational and community problems not only as results of individuals' behavior or of forces in the social context, but of the combination of the two. The book also has a potential to help users of OD services (human resource managers and community leaders) to understand what to expect from OD consultants and how to identify, hire and use the resources OD offers.

What Is Not in the Book?

This book does not provide OD training. One cannot learn how to become an OD consultant just by reading a book, not even this book. Reading a book can be an inspiration for those interested in engaging in OD projects, like HR managers. No more than that. As I have noted, to facilitate OD projects one should participate in formal and practical training.

Furthermore, acquiring OD skills entails knowledge that is not in the book. Part of this knowledge is within the boundaries of OD's field and part is outside the field. For example, how do human resource departments work? What are organizational cultures and organizational strategy? How can we relate to questions of gender and ethnicity in organizations? What are the social, cultural and economic structures of the social fields (local community, city, state, global system) where the consulting takes place?

A Few Words About Methodology

Schein reports on a meeting of teachers of organizational psychology and sociology held at the Harvard Business School in 1983 (Schein, 1987a). The participants lectured and openly discussed their research and practical consulting experience.

During the discussions, one of the participants asked the rest of the group to share the way they integrate their research findings with teaching. The common answer was that in the classroom participants relied more on their consulting experience and less on research findings. According to Schein, a significant number of the participants agreed that theoretical materials based on research, those that appear in academic journals, encourage thinking, give context to practical experience, but rarely enrich the instruction. The empirical basis of their lessons, the one they have most trusted and believed to be happening in organizations, instead, was their own consulting experience. Participants admitted that the materials they read in the journals are not "having the ring of truth" (p. 13) and largely they do not represent the entire organizational reality.

At last, two camps formed the meeting. One camp consisted of those who rely only on research and do not feel the need to assimilate into the organizations' reality. The second camp relied on knowledge gathered in consulting experience and in various types of fieldwork. The author of this book belongs to the second group, those who do research-based practice, who are commonly referred to as "scholar-practitioners" (Astley and Zammuto, 1992; Kram, Wasserman and Yip, 2012; Rosile and Boje, 1996). As a scholar-practitioner involved both in the worlds of academia and practice, I change the accepted order that views practice as a result of theory by granting practical knowledge independent and legitimate status (Van de Ven and Johnson, 2006). Following Mary Ellen Kondrat (1992, p. 239), I believe that "when this status is granted, the practical takes its place alongside the scientific as constitutive elements of professional knowledge".

All the empirical materials in this book are from my consulting work; thus, they have both strengths and limitations. On the one hand, my active involvement in organizations' daily life makes me very familiar with the organizational reality, with its cultures and politics as well as with other aspects of its everyday social dynamics (Kuna, 2014). However, it is clear to me that my personal involvement makes it difficult to meet strict tests of objectivity and reliability. For example, I sometimes find that my close personal relations with figures in the organization can influence my position on a given issue. This bias manifests itself mainly in situations of conflict between individuals (and groups) and in dramatic organizational changes that affect the organization's stability and especially, the future of powerless employees. In a situation like this, very often my sociological habitus generates a spontaneous reaction that positions me on the side of the powerless.

The Book's Chapters

In the following chapter, I present an overview of the OD field. Although there are many excellent overviews, I choose to include this overview in order to highlight and put in context the contribution of the HOOD to the OD field and vice-versa. In chapter three, I present the HOOD's theoretical infrastructure by applying the concept of habitus and other Bourdieu's concepts (capital, field, doxa, strategies and symbolic violence) to a case study from my consulting experience. In chapter four, I use the case study presented in chapter three to show how the HOOD re/roots with OD's original democratic and humanistic values and with its position between organizations and society. Based on a new case study from my consulting experience, in chapter five I illustrate how the HOOD comprehends processes of resistance to change (RTC). In chapter six, I use an example from a highly skilled surgical department of a big hospital in Israel to show how the HOOD helped me and my consultees define and effectively cope with the department's problem of intensive conflictual interactions. In chapter seven, I show how the HOOD uses OD's traditional practices and techniques to achieve its objectives. In chapter eight, I discuss possible contributions of the HOOD to the production of a critical perspective that is able to apply moral and effective organization development and change processes that position the HOOD in between organizations and society. Chapter nine summarizes the book by juxtaposing the habitus with both the individual (self) and cultural orientations in order to show the advantage of using the concept of habitus for understanding and implementing change processes. I end the chapter by offering possibilities for further conceptual and practical development of HOOD projects.

Notes

1 I disagree with those who contend that OD's focus on problem solving has reached a dead end or should be replaced (e.g., Bushe and Marshak, 2009; Marshak, 2005; Voronov and Woodworth, 2012). Rather, I believe that OD as clearly defined by early scholar-practitioners is, and should continue to be, primarily a problem-solving approach and a helping profession focusing

on consultees' inner worlds in order to help them understand and cope with organization problems.

2 One should remember that not all psychological discourses reduce the process of organizational change to the individual level (Fincham and Clark, 2002; Bradford and Burke, 2005; Bradford and Porras, 2005). "Organizational psychology", for example, offers rich conceptual frameworks and metaphors for organization-wide planning and strategy (Taylor, 1992). Another example is the search of organizational psychology for the effects of unconscious behavior on organizations (see Kets de Vries, 2003). Organizational psychologists who deal with planning and strategy or unconscious, then, do not reduce the organization to the individual level; rather, they use psychological metaphors to represent and analyze the organization as a whole. The criticism should be therefore, and is in this book, not of the use of psychological terms, but of the use individually oriented OD makes of the discourse of therapeutic psychology, that attempts to change organizations by changing individuals. To make it clear, in this book I relate only to the therapeutic psychological discourse as it has been integrated (Schein, 1987) into and criticized by (Voronov and Woodworth, 2012) OD writers. Moreover, in this book I do not pretend to pose sociology against psychology. Rather, I try to enrich the OD field with Bourdieu's sociological concepts that can consider the organizations' social context and the place of individuals in that context.

Bibliography

Alvesson, M. and H. Willmott (1996). *Making Sense of Management: A Critical Introduction*. London: Sage Publications.

Argyris, C. (1972). *The Applicability of Organizational Sociology*. Cambridge, MA: Cambridge University Press.

Astley, W. G. and R. F. Zammuto (1992). Organization science, managers, and language games. *Organization Science,* 3(4), 443–460.

Bartunek, J. M. (2008). You're an organization development practitioner-scholar: Can you contribute to organizational theory? *Organization Management Journal,* 5(1), 6–16.

Battilana, J. (2006). Agency and institutions: The enabling role of individuals' social position. *Organization,* 13(5), 653–676.

Battilana, J., M. Anteby and M. Sengul (2010). The circulation of ideas across academic communities: When locals re-import exported ideas. *Organization Studies,* 31(6), 695–713.

Beer, M., R. A. Eisenstat and B. Spector (1990). Why change programs don't produce change. *Harvard Business Review,* 68(6), 4–12.

Bierema, L. L. (2010). *Implementing a Critical Approach to Organization Development*. Malabar, FL: Krieger.

Boje, M. D. (2012). Postscript. In D. M. Boje, B. Burnes and J. Hassard (Eds.), *The Routledge Companion to Organizational Change*. (pp. 598–601). London and New York: Routledge.

Bort, S. and A. Kieser (2011). Fashion in organization theory: An empirical analysis of the diffusion of theoretical concepts. *Organization Studies,* 32(5), 655–681.

Bourdieu, P. (1977). *Outline of a Theory of Practice*. Cambridge, MA: Cambridge University Press.

Bourdieu, P. (1988). *Homo Academicus*. Stanford, CA: Stanford University Press.

Bourdieu, P. (1989). Social space and symbolic power. *Sociological Theory*, 7(1), 14–25.

Bourdieu, P. (1990). *The Logic of Practice*. Stanford, CA: Stanford University Press.

Bourdieu, P. (1998). *On Television and Journalism*. (Translated: Priscilla Parkhurst and Ferguson). London: Pluto.

Bourdieu, P. and L. Wacquant (1992). *An Invitation to Reflexive Sociology*. Chicago, IL and London: University of Chicago Press.

Bradford, D. L. and W. W. Burke (2005). The future of OD? In D. L. Bradford and W. W. Burke (Eds.), *Reinventing Organization Development: New Approaches to Change in Organizations*. (pp. 43–64). San Francisco, CA: Pfeiffer.

Bradford, D. L. and J. I. Porras (2005). A historical view of the future of OD: An interview with J. I. Porras. In D. L. Bradford and W. W. Burke (Eds.), *Reinventing Organization Development: New Approaches to Change in Organizations*. (pp. 43–64). San Francisco, CA: Pfeiffer.

Bruhn, J. G. and H. M. Rebach (2007). *Sociological Practice: Intervention and Social Change*. New York: Springer.

Bruhn, J. G. and H. M. Rebach (Eds.) (2012). *Handbook of Clinical Sociology*. New York: Springer Science & Business Media.

Bunker, B. B., B. T. Alban and R. J. Lewicki (2004). Ideas in currency and OD practice: Has the well gone dry? *The Journal of Applied Behavioral Science*, 40(4), 403–422.

Burnes, B. (2012a). Introduction. In D. M. Boje, B. Burnes and J. Hassard (Eds.), *The Routledge Companion to Organizational Change*. (pp. 11–14). London and New York: Routledge.

Burnes, B. (2012b). Understanding the emergent approach to change. In D. M. Boje, B. Burnes and J. Hassard (Eds.), *The Routledge Companion to Organizational Change*. (pp. 133–145). London and New York: Routledge.

Burnes, B. and D. Bargal (2017). Kurt Lewin: 70 years on. *Journal of Change Management*, 17(2), 91–100.

Burnes, B. and B. Cooke (2012). Review article: The past, present and future of organization development: Taking the long view. *Human Relations*, 65(11), 1395–1429.

Bushe, G. R. and R. J. Marshak (2009). Revisioning organization development: Diagnostic and dialogic premises and patterns of practice. *The Journal of Applied Behavioral Science*, 45(3), 348–368.

Church, A. H., J. Waclawski and W. Siegal (1996). Will the real OD practitioner please stand up? A call for change in the field. *Organization Development Journal*, 14(2), 5–14.

Coghlan, D. (2012). Organization development and action research: Then and now. In D. M. Boje, B. Burnes and J. Hassard (Eds.), *The Routledge Companion to Organizational Change*. (pp. 45–58). London and New York: Routledge.

Costea, B., N. Crump and K. Amiridis (2008). Managerialism, the therapeutic habitus and the self in contemporary organizing. *Human Relations*, 61(5), 661–685.

Deer, C. (2008). *Reflexivity, Pierre Bourdieu: Key Concepts*. (p. 195). London and New York: Routledge.

Dobbin, F. (2008). The poverty of organizational theory: Comment on: "Bourdieu and organizational analysis". *Theory and Society*, 37, 53–63.

Emirbayer, M. and V. Johnson (2008). Bourdieu and organizational analysis. *Theory and Society*, 37(1), 1–44.

Emirbayer, M. and E. M. Williams (2005). Bourdieu and social work. *Social Service Review*, 79(4), 689–724.

Everett, J. (2002). Organizational research and the praxeology of Pierre Bourdieu. *Organizational Research Methods*, 5(1), 56–80.

Fincham, R. and T. Clark (2002). Introduction: The emergence of critical perspective on consulting. In T. Clark and R. Fincham (Eds.), *Critical Consulting: New Perspectives on the Management Advice Industry*. (pp. 1–18). Oxford: Blackwell.

Ford, J. D., L. W. Ford and A. D'Amelio (2008). Resistance to change: The rest of the story. *The Academy of Management Review*, 33(2), 362–377.

Forson, C., M. Özbilgin, M. B. Ozturk and A. Abu Tatli (2014). Multi-level approaches to entrepreneurship and small business research-transcending dichotomies with Bourdieu. In E. Chell and M. Karatas-Ozkan (Eds.), *Handbook of Research on Small Business and Entrepreneurship*. (pp. 54–69). Cheltenham: Edward Elgar Publishing.

Foster, S. W. (1986). Reading Pierre Bourdieu. *Cultural Anthropology*, 1(1), 103–110.

French, W. L. and C. H. Bell (1999). *Organization Development: Behavioral Science Interventions for Organization Improvement*. Norwood, NJ: Prentice Hall.

Friedman, V. J. (2011). Revisiting social space: Relational thinking about organizational change. In *Research in Organizational Change and Development*. (pp. 233–257). Bingley: Emerald Group Publishing.

Garrett, P. M. (2007). Making social work more Bourdieusian: Why the social professions should critically engage with the work of Pierre Bourdieu. *Journal of Social Work*, 10(2), 225–243.

Greiner, L. E. and T. G. Cummings (2005). OD: Wanted more alive than dead! In D. L. Bradford and W. W. Burke (Eds.), *Reinventing Organization Development: New Approaches to Change in Organizations*. (pp. 87–112). San Francisco, CA: Pfeiffer.

Grenfell, M. (2010). Being critical: The practical logic of Bourdieu's metanoia. *Critical Studies in Education*, 51(1), 85–99.

Illouz, E. (2007). *Cold Intimacies: The Making of Emotional Capitalism*. London: Polity Press.

Jackall, R. (1988). Moral mazes: The world of corporate managers. *International Journal of Politics, Culture, and Society*, 1(4), 598–614.

Katz, D. and R. L. Kahn (1966). *The Social Psychology of Organizations*. New York: Wiley.

Kerr, R. and S. Robinson (2009). The hysteresis effect as creative adaption of the habitus: Dissent and transition to the 'corporate' in post-soviet Ukraine. *Organization*, 16(6), 829–853.

Kets de Vries, M. F. R. (2003). *Organizations on the Couch: A Clinical Perspective on Organizational Dynamics*. Retrieved from www.insead.edu/faculty research/research/doc.cfm?did=1321

Kitchin, P. J. and P. D. Howe (2013). How can the social theory of Pierre Bourdieu assist sport management research? *Sport Management Review*, 16(2), 123–134.

Kondrat, M. E. (1992). Reclaiming the practical: Formal and substantive rationality in social work practice. *Social Service Review*, 66(2), 237–255.

Kram, K. E., I. C. Wasserman and J. Yip (2012). Metaphors of identity and professional practice: Learning from the scholar–practitioner. *The Journal of Applied Behavioral Science*, 48(3), 304–341.

Kuna, S. (2014). *Liquid Professionalism: A Critical View of Management Consulting*. Tel-Aviv: Resling.

Lahire, B. (2002). How to keep a critical tradition alive: A tribute to Pierre Bourdieu. *Review of International Political Economy*, 9(4), 595–600.

Lapidot-Lefler, N., V. J. Friedman, D. Arieli, N. Haj, I. Sykes and N. N. Kais (2015). Social space and field as constructs for evaluating social inclusion. *New Directions for Evaluation*, 2015(146), 33–43.

Lawrence, P. R. and J. W. Lorsch (1969). *Developing Organizations: Diagnosis and* Action. Menlo Park, CA: Addison-Wesley.

Leander, A. (2001). Review essay: Pierre Bourdieu on economics. *Review of International Political Economy*, 8(2), 344–353.

Lewin, K. (1939). Field theory and experiment in social psychology: Concepts and methods. *American Journal of Sociology*, 44(6), 868–896.

Lippitt, G. and R. Lippitt (1978). *The Consulting Process in Action*. San Diego, CA: University Associates.

Marshak, R. J. (2005). Contemporary challenges to the philosophy and practice of organization development. In D. L. Bradford and W. W. Burke (Eds.), *Reinventing Organization Development: New Approaches to Change in Organizations*. (pp. 19–42). San Francisco, CA: Pfeiffer.

Maton, K. (2014). Habitus. In *Pierre Bourdieu: Key Concepts*. (second edition). (pp. 48–64). London and New York: Routledge.

Meyer, R. E. and E. Boxenbaum (2010). Exploring European-ness in organization research. *Organization Studies,* 31(6), 737–755.

Nathan, J. D. and A. Whatley (2006). Critical theory: A means for transforming organization development. *Organization Development Journal*, 24(2), 61–68.

Nicoll, D. (1999). Opening up OD values to 21st century realities. *OD Practitioner*, 31(2), 5.

Oakes, L. S., B. Townley and Cooper, D. J. (1998). Business planning as pedagogy: Language and control in a changing institutional field. *Administrative Science Quarterly*, 43, 257–292.

Ottaway, R. N. (1983). The change agent: A taxonomy in relation to the change process. *Human Relations*, 36(4), 361–392.

Özbilgin, M., A. Tatli and M. Queen (2005). Book review essay: Understanding Bourdieu's contribution to organization and management studies. *The Academy of Management Review*, 30(4), 855–869.

Raedeke, A. H., J. J. Green, S. S. Hodge and C. Valdivia (2003). Farmers, the practice of farming and the future of agroforestry: An application of Bourdieu's concepts of field and habitus. *Rural Sociology*, 68(1), 64–86.

Reynolds, M. and R. Vince (2004). Critical management education and action-based learning: Synergies and contradictions. *Academy of Management Learning & Education*, 3(4), 442–456.

Rosile, G. A. and D. M. Boje (1996). Pedagogy for the postmodern management classroom: Greenback company. In D. M. Boje, R. P. Gephart and

T. J. Thatchenkery (Eds.), *Postmodern Management and Organization Theory*. (pp. 225–250). London: Sage Publications.

Schein, E. H. (1969). *Process Consultation: Its Role in Organization Development*. Reading, MA: Addison-Wesley.

Schein, E. H. (1987a). *Process Consultation: Lessons for Managers and Consultants*. (Vol. 2). Reading, MA: Addison-Wesley.

Schein, E. H. (1987b). The clinical perspective in fieldwork, In *Qualitative Research Methods Series*. (Vol. 5). Newbury Park: Sage Publications.

Schein, E. H. (1999). *Process Consultation Revisited: Building the Helping Relationship*. Reading, MA: Addison-Wesley.

Schein, E. H. (2005). Organization development: A wedding of anthropology and Organization therapy. In D. L. Bradford and W. W. Burke (Eds.), *Reinventing Organization Development: New Approaches to Change in Organizations*. (pp. 131–144). San Francisco, CA: Pfeiffer.

Schein, E. H. (2009). *Helping: How to Offer, Give, and Receive Help*. San Francisco, CA: Berrett-Koehler.

Shimoni, B. (2017). What is resistance to change? A habitus-oriented approach. *Academy of Management Perspectives*, 31(4), 1–14.

Sieweke, J. (2014). Pierre Bourdieu in management and organization studies: A citation context analysis and discussion of contributions. *Scandinavian Journal of Management*, 30(4), 532–543.

Swartz, D. (1997). *Culture and Power: The Sociology of Pierre Bourdieu*. Chicago, IL and London: University of Chicago Press.

Tatli, A., M. Özbilgin and M. Karatas-Ozkan (2015). Introduction: Management and organization studies meet Pierre Bourdieu. In A. Tatli, M. Özbilgin and M. Karatas-Ozkan (Eds.), *Pierre Bourdieu, Organization, and Management*. London and New York: Routledge.

Taylor, R. N. (1992). Strategic decision-making. In M. D. Dunnete and L. M. Houge (Eds.), *Handbook of Industrial and Organizational Psychology*. (second edition). (Vol. 3, pp. 961–1008). Palo Alto, CA: Consulting Psychologists Press.

Tenkasi, V., R. Rami and G. W. Hai (2008). Following the second legacy of Aristotle: The scholar-practitioner as an Epistemic Technician. In A. B. Shani, S. A. Mohrman, W. A. Pasmore, B. Stymne and N. Adler (Eds.), *Handbook of Collaborative Management Research*. (pp. 49–72). Los Angeles, CA: Sage Publications.

Vandenberghe, F. (1999). "The Real is Relational": An epistemological analysis of Pierre Bourdieu's generative structuralism. *Sociological Theory*, 17(1), 32–67.

Van de Ven, A. H. and P. E. Johnson (2006). Knowledge for theory and practice. *Academy of Management Review*, 31(4), 802–821.

Vaughan, D. (2008). Bourdieu and organizations: The empirical challenge. *Theory and Society*, 37(1), 65–81.

Voronov, M. (2005). Should critical management studies and organization development collaborate? Invitation to a contemplation. *Organization Management Journal*, 2(1), 4–26.

Voronov, M. (2008). Toward engaged critical management studies. *Organization*, 15(6), 939–945.

Voronov, M. and W. P. Woodworth (2012). OD discourse and domination. In D. M. Boje, B. Burnes and J. Hassard (Eds.), *The Routledge Companion to Organizational Change*. (pp. 440–455). London and New York: Routledge.

Wacquant, L. J. (1989). Towards a reflexive sociology: A workshop with Pierre Bourdieu. *Sociological Theory*, 7(1), 26–63.

Worley, C. G. and A. E. Feyerherm (2003). Reflections on the future of organization development. *The Journal of Applied Behavioral Science*, 39(1), 97–115.

Zand, D. E. (2010). An OD odyssey: In search of inward light. *The Journal of Applied Behavioral Science*, 46(4), 424–435.

2 A Short Overview of the OD Field

1940s–1950s: Kurt Lewin and OD's Ideological, Theoretical and Practical Foundations

Kurt Lewin and the Connecticut Seminar

On a winter's day in 1946, the Connecticut Committee for Racial Relations in the United States contacted social psychologist Kurt Lewin to arrange a training workshop for community leaders on how to deal with racial and religious discrimination in housing, education and work (Freedman, 1999). Fifty community leaders, half of whom were Black and Jewish, participated in the summer of 1946 in a two-day workshop in New Britain, Connecticut. Although the name "Organization Development" was not familiar to the workshop organizers or to other participants, it was probably the first significant determination of the philosophical, theoretical and practical principles of the OD field. The purpose of the workshop was to improve ethnic relations, especially between Jews and Blacks. However, the workshop's main contribution was apparently in the development of the participants' self-awareness and knowledge of group dynamics (Coghlan and Jacobs, 2005).

The workshop was a sort of laboratory for the implementation of research ideas developed in Kurt Lewin's studies on democratic, autocratic and laissez-faire leadership styles (Lewin, Lippitt, and White, 1939). Lewin, who escaped Nazi Germany in the 1930s (many of his family did not survive the Holocaust), devoted his professional life to the development of social and cultural alternatives to Nazi totalitarianism and collectivistic obedience. His main belief, which later became one of the important principles in the OD field, was that democracy is the most effective framework for dealing with social conflicts. In his research, he showed that democracy and participation have achieved better results than autocracy and insisted that autocratic leaders who wish to succeed should change their behavior and develop democratic systems of participation. To a great extent, OD's democratic and humanistic values are a direct result of Lewin's personal experience of the Holocaust.

Table 2.1 The source of consultees' thinking and behavior

Period	Content	Contributors
1940–1950s *In the interaction between the individual and the social context*	"To explain social behavior, it is necessary to represent the structure of the total situation and the distribution of the forces in it" (Lewin, 1939, p. 868).	Lewin, 1939; Lewin, Lippitt, and White, 1939.
1960s *Within the individual*	"[I]n the early 1960s groups (T-groups, sensitivity training groups, encounter groups) were being used primarily to transform people . . . I think the basic belief at the time was that OD processes could really transform people, make them psychologically healthier" (Bradford and Porras, 2005, pp. 45–46).	French, 1977; Lippitt and Lippitt, 1978; Schein, 1969, 1987, 1999.
1970s–1980s *In the social context*	"In fact, individual behavior is powerfully shaped by the organizational roles that people play. The most effective way to change behavior, therefore, is to put people into a new roles, responsibilities, and relationships on them. This creates a situation that, in a sense, 'forces' new attitudes and behaviors on people" (Beer, Eisenstat, and Spector, 1990, p. 159).	Beer, Eisenstat, and Spector, 1990; Daft and Weick, 1986; Katz and Kahn, 1966.
1990s–current *In the social interaction*	"In terms of generative dialogue, then, the central focus is on those kinds of dialogic moves that may bring realities and ethics into being and bind them to particular patterns of action" (Gergen, Gergen, and Barrett, 2004, p. 37).	Boyd and Bright, 2007; Bushe and Kassam, 2005; Cooperrider and Sekerka, 2006; Gergen, 1978.
HOOD *In the dialectical relations between individuals and social structures—in the habitus*	Consultees' thinking and behavior is produced by social agents' habitus, historically developed in constant interactions between human agents and social structures in a given social field (Shimoni, 2017a, 2017b).	

Kurt Lewin's Field Theory

Lewin, then, positioned himself in the space between organizations and society. Specifically, he saw his research and group workshops as a theoretical and practical infrastructure for change in both organizations and society. In his field theory, which he based on both physics and the Gestalt school of psychology, Lewin assumes that personal behavior should be appraised in the social context (Bargal, 2011). In a formulation he offers, behavior (B) is a function of the interaction between the person (P) and the environment (E): $B = f(P, E)$

The Training Group (T-Group)

The first T-Group took place in Bethel, Maine, in the summer of 1947 in the spirit of Kurt Lewin's pioneering workshop in Connecticut. The T-Group used the practice of group dynamic to develop participants' personal and social skills as a way to improve their performance in the community and at work. T-Group workshops largely reflect the position accepted today in the various consulting professions in psychology, social work and clinical sociology, according to which reflection and self-discovery (among consultees and consultants) are a necessity for personal growth and behavioral change.

The T-Group's organizers believed that training that deals with human relations and focuses on emotions and other personal concerns is a more valuable form of education than the lecture model (French, 1969, p. 489). Thus, the T-Group (often called "sensitivity training") was not structured and did not have a defined agenda so it could openly and freely enables participants to develop insights into themselves and others. The instructors facilitated the T-Group in accordance with democratic and humanistic values to allow participants voluntarily to use these insights to improve their interpersonal skills and as a basis for change in the community and in the organizations from which they came (Burke, 2008). According to Warner Burke (1992, pp. 179–180),

> This method [sensitivity training] of education and change has humanistic value orientation, the belief that it is worthwhile for people to have the opportunity throughout their lives to learn and develop personally toward a full realization and actualization of individual potentials.

According to Burnes and Cooke (2012), the increasing use of T-Groups has led to the establishment of at least two components that over time have become central in the OD field. First, it increased participants' sensitivity to interpersonal processes as a way to solve human problems, regardless of the subject they are discussing and of the problem on the agenda. Second, the T-Group has raised awareness of learning that uses direct interpersonal confrontation and open feedback in which participants live the group processes and deeply experience self-learning, with the pain and pleasure that involves. Specifically, the assumption was that in effective groups the voice of all group members should be heard.

The T-Group of the 1940s and 1950s thus embodied Lewin's humanistic and democratic values and his central assumption that personal behavior should always be considered in relation to others.

Action Research

In his research on minority relations and group dynamics, Kurt Lewin (1946) developed "action research" as a diagnostic tool for organized and planned action aimed at identifying, defining and solving problems. It would be based on systemic social philosophy and on democratic and human values. Lewin argued that conducting organizational change through action research would be effective only if it occurs at the group level and allows a common process of discourse, debate and experiment involving many participants (Bargal, Gold, and Lewin, 1992). Lewin translated this argument into research-based applied practice in which consultants, managers and employees together take part.

Action research thus is a process in which consultants provide tools for solving problems directly by members of the organization. Lewin chose the name *action research*, since for him the aim of community and organizational interventions is never the research itself but the social action the intervention involves. Specifically, believing in democracy and cooperation and in the power of the group to allow creative and innovative thinking, Lewin thought that the active social and cultural dynamic that action research generates would be as important as its measurable results. For him, action research projects are most importantly a tool for the production of dialogue and shared understanding of the context within which behaviors occur (Burnes and Cooke, 2012).

The 1960s: The Psychologists' Era and the Individualistic Orientation

It seems safe to say that the individually oriented OD, at least partially derived from modern western social structure. In this structure, the individual is an autonomic subject, entitled to self-expression and self-actualization and is therefore the main source of meanings, values and practical norms (Gergen, Gergen, and Barrett, 2004). We can find examples of the location of meanings and values in the individual self in fields such as education, law and labor. The labor market largely serves as a place for individuals' self-expression and actualization (Rose, 1991). A common belief about the western labor market is that individuals' potential can reach actualization if organizations keep improving individuals' psychological dispositions and interpersonal skills such as emotional control, self-performance, self-consciousness, effective interpersonal communication and active listening (Costea, Crump, and Amiridis, 2008, p. 665).

The individualistic orientation developed in the modern western social structure closely corresponds with the US's post-WWII social structure. The dominant properties of this social structure, which is based heavily on the individually oriented psychological perspective, cherished ideas such as freedom and equity and emphasized notions like self-development and growth, self-expression and self-actualization (Burnes and Cooke, 2012).

It seems that the most practical expression of these ideas in the OD field in the US in the 1960s is the individually oriented post-Lewinian T-Groups that focused mainly on developing participants' insights into their own and others' psychological dispositions (French, 1977, p. 489). At that time (1960s), it was widely accepted that the T-Groups would serve more as frameworks for personal care and development and less as laboratories for social change (Bradford and Porras, 2005). Following the extensive entry of consultants with backgrounds in psychology and psychiatry, the T-Groups largely abandoned a systemic perspective in favor of a perspective focused on the individual. Participants' social background and the consideration of the group as a system have become secondary to ideas and practices such as personal growth and self-development. T-Groups have largely become sites for "therapy for normals" (Schein, 2005, p. 132).

According to Edgar Schein (1969, 2005), OD's strong tendency to place the individual at the center of the change process in the 1960s emerged mainly from a humanistic belief that grew in response to Taylor's Scientific Management approach, which focused mainly on the structural and technical aspects of the organization. Taylorism referred to people as a natural part of the organization structure or technology, says Schein (1969, p. 11), while ignoring the participants "personality", their personal motivations and needs. This individual orientated approach, according to Frank Friedlander and Dave Brown (1974, p. 325), appears in many aspects of the consulting process, such as interpersonal communication, problem-solving and decision-making. Its roots are in the academic disciplines of psychology, social psychology and anthropology and "in the applied disciplines of group dynamics and the human relations movement". The individually oriented approach, according to Friedlander and Brown (p. 325), "tends to value human fulfillment highly and to expect improved organizational performance to follow on improved human functioning and processes".

Individually oriented OD, then, reflects a dominant tendency in the 1960s to put "the individual before the organization", says Larry Greiner (1972; Greiner and Cummings, 2005, p. 93). That is, it focuses on personal skills such as leadership style and team development and not on the development of the organization as one whole. In an interview with David Bradford, Jerry Porras (Bradford and Porras, 2005) attributes this trend mainly to the intensive integration of psychologists into the OD field in the 1950s and 1960s. Organizational psychologists, he says, were trained to see internal motives as the main reason for individuals' behavior and therefore were busy developing ways to change people. Thus, OD fell into a "reductionist trap", according to Bradford and Burke (2005, p. 199), in which OD tried to change organizations by changing individuals (see also Bradford and Porras, 2005; Fincham and Clark, 2002.

1970s–1980s: The Structural Orientation and the Consultants' Era

In the 1970s, the ground was laid for a return to Lewin's (1939) systemic approach that sees the social context as highly important for the understanding of individuals and group behavior. Richard Daft and Karl Weick (1986), for instance, suggest that organizations be viewed as interpretive or cognitive systems with a "collective memory". Interpretation, according to the two researchers, is an act of individuals, but organizational interpretation is more than interpretation of individuals. Individuals come and go, but organizations stay; they retain knowledge, behavior, norms, values and mental systems that act as "behavior-oriented structures". Michael Beer, Russell Eisenstat, and Bert Spector (1990) argue that most organizational change programs are unsuccessful because they are guided by an erroneous change theory; accordingly, changing individuals' behavior should begin with the knowledge and attitudes individuals hold. Beer, Eisenstat, and Spector (1990) think that individuals' thoughts and behavior are strongly shaped by the system in which they operate, especially their organizational role in that system. Thus, the most effective way to change behavior is to integrate people into a new organizational context that will impose new roles, responsibilities and relationships on them.

It seems that the first to offer a significant systemic view that sees organizations as part of a wider social context were Daniel Katz and Robert Kahn (1966), who developed the open system approach. According to Katz and Kahn, the main mistake in dealing with organizational change in the 1960s is the focus on self-development practices meant to directly improve participants' behavior, thus seeing the organization as a closed system not affected by the environment. Organizations, like humans, they claim, are open systems that exchange information and resources with the environment in which they operate. Organizations cannot control their behavior fully because behaviors are always subject to the influence of external forces such as availability of raw materials, customer requirements, competition and legal arrangements. Understanding the influence of these forces on the organization is crucial for appreciating its internal behaviors.

A specific form of the open system approach is what Friedlander and Brown (1974, pp. 320–321) define as "techno-structural approaches". Such approaches to OD "refer to theories of and interventions into the technology (e.g., task methods and processes) and the structure (e.g., the relationships, roles, arrangements) of the organization". Specifically, the aim of techno-structural change interventions is to affect both work processes and relationships. The techno-structural perspective includes approaches such as "job design and enlargement" and "job enrichment", which in general seek to change and improve the working context, the "work itself" (Hackman and Oldham, 1975). Changing the work itself by building in greater variety, discretion, feedback, identity and responsibility for whole-task completion, then, will increase satisfaction and performance.

The techno-structural approach also includes "socio-technical systems" (Trist, 1981). Socio-technical systems were initiated by the Tavistock Institute in England to combine the technological and the social aspects of work units. Change interventions driven by the socio-technical approach focus on both the technical aspects of the job and the social structures that support it.

Job design and enlargement, job enrichment and socio-technical systems are largely a reaction to and an emergence from two earlier yet still-current approaches to change. The first uses scientific management and industrial engineering to focus on the physical context and the physiological requirements of workers. The second approach uses psychology and social psychology to focus on relationships and personal needs. They "criticize the physical approach for treating social groups and individuals mechanistically, and criticize the psychological approach for ignoring the technology of the organization or treating it as unchangeable" (Friedlander and Brown, 1974, pp. 320–321). As an alternative, the three approaches (job design and enlargement, job enrichment and socio-technical systems) consider equally both the physical and the personal and social sides of the organization and search for the interaction between the two.

In the 1980s, the OD field was dominated less by academics and more by consultants who recognized that in a global economic slowdown (characterized by the closing of large-scale factories and mass layoffs), in which decisions are made from above, a democratic OD which seeks to initiate changes from below is inappropriate. Organizations were looking for new ideas focused on making economic profit and OD consultants responded appropriately by developing practices and values "toward achieving business effectiveness and outcomes over traditional humanistic values" (Anderson, 2015, p. 49). OD in the 1980s thus shifted the focus of change from individuals and small groups to the economic and systemic level. "Organization culture" and "organizational learning" approaches are two significant examples (Freedman, 1999; Sanzgiri and Gottlieb, 1992).

Organization culture, as commonly perceived by mainstream OD, enables managers to shape and control individuals and groups, emotions, perspectives and behaviors (Kunda, 2009). By promoting organizational identity and sense of pride, the organization's culture is a vital resource for increasing effectiveness and profitability (Deal and Kennedy, 1982; Peters and Waterman, 1982). The organization learning approach assumes that understanding organizational problems, for instance, requires looking beyond the mistakes of individuals. It requires learning the hidden social and structural elements at the organization level that shape participants' thoughts and behavior, and the conditions under which their behavior is likely to occur (Senge, 1991). Organization learning encourages personal learning and redefining structure, culture, role planning and organizational mental models that drive thought and behavior (Burke, 2008).

1990s–2000s: The Scholar-Practitioners' Era and the Postmodern Constructionist Orientation

The Postmodern Perspective

In the last three decades, OD scholars and practitioners have begun to develop a new body of knowledge that deals with organizational change from a postmodern perspective (Bushe and Marshak, 2008). The postmodern perspective is holistic and contextual and thus views organizations as parts of changing social environments. Change processes from this perspective should not be thought of as rational processes and they cannot be fully *planned*, as traditional OD would do, but rather are ongoing processes influenced constantly by changes in culture, power and politics. Despite the fact that the postmodern approach has been, and still is, very attractive to researchers, Burnes and Cook (2012) say that OD consultants have not fully adopted it. They see the postmodern perspective as very strong in analysis but weak in implementation; it is important for understanding but not for changing organizations.

The rapid diffusion of "Appreciative Inquiry" (AI) and the "Dialogic OD" (DOD), developed at the end of the 1980s, enabled postmodern thinking to acquire practical sense and meaning. AI and DOD, which Gervase Bushe and Robert Marshak (2009) see as a philosophical, theoretical and practical alternative to traditional OD, view organizations as socially constructed. Organizations are not situations in which the source of consultees' thinking and behavior is *either* in the individual (1960s) *or* in the social context (1970s–1980s), but are both-end situations constructed by individuals in their daily interactions. Consulting interventions in the spirit of AI and DOD have taken place in organizations such as Amnesty international, Greenpeace and Deloitte (Cram, 2010).

I totally agree with Warner Burke (2010, p. 1) who claims, "Essentially, and perhaps arguably, there has been no innovation in the social technology of organization development (OD) since appreciative inquiry originated in 1987". The dominance of AI in the OD field, I believe, requires not only a presentation of AI (and DOD) but also positioning HOOD deeply in reference to the two approaches. This is what I do in the next part of this chapter.

Appreciative Inquiry (AI)

AI applies postmodern and constructional ideas developed by Kenneth Gergen, especially in his article "Toward a Generative Theory" (Gergen, 1978). Gergen, a social psychologist and organizational consultant is considered to have made a breakthrough in the development of the social construction approach in social psychology. He argues that the most important thing social science can do is give us new ways to think about social structures and institutions and to maintain creative and unconventional thinking that will lead to new possibilities of action. AI attempts to produce these new ideas, images, theories and models. According to Gergen, success in the implementation of AI produces individual, group and organizational action that leads to a better future (Bushe, 2007).

In the late 1980s, Gergen's theoretical writings served David Cooperrider in a series of publications, including "Appreciative Inquiry in Organizational Life", the important article he published with Suresh Srivastava (Cooperrider and Srivastva, 1987), to lay the theoretical and practical foundations of AI. Cooperrider reminds OD scholars and practitioners that in processes of research and consulting reality is shaped by the way the questions are asked (Cram, 2010). In organizations, as in any social system, according to Cooperrider, prophecies tend to fulfill themselves, thus questions highlighting negative experiences, which look for problems, will define organizations as needing to be cured. Questions about participants' positive experiences and organizational success, on the other hand, will define organizations as sites of capabilities and will result in positive change.

OD scholars and practitioners who are interested in bringing positive change to organizations should therefore express appreciation for participants' experience. They invite participants to talk about the organization's success and about any other experience that has brought them pleasure and satisfaction. Cooperrider borrows the concept of appreciation from the *appreciative eye* in art, which assumes that every piece of art has beauty. Similarly, every organization has beauty, regardless of its current state. If OD consultants can find the beauty, they can help members of the organization to find it and use it to imagine and build a new and better future (Gergen, McNamee, and Barret, 2001).

For AI, then, organizations are not problems OD consultants need to solve and employees are not a workforce they need to master. Organizations are "centers of abilities" and of interpersonal relationships that can stimulate a vision of a better future (Gergen, Gergen, and Barrett, 2004). In this sense, AI is a generative practice, capable of engendering new ideas and action in the social world. It is a transformative practice, which creates new experiences (Boyd and Bright, 2007). According to French and Bell (1999, p. 208), an appreciative belief in the positive power of individuals and collectives assumes that the organization is a "miracle to be embraced" rather than "a problem to be solved".

Dialogic OD (DOD)

The theoretical, philosophical and practical principles of AI furnish many new approaches to organizational change, often described as Dialogic OD (DOD) (Bushe and Marshak, 2009, 2013; Marshak and Bushe, 2013).

The dialogic approaches explore ways to promote dialogue and conversation, assuming that changing conversations will lead to organizational change (Bushe, 2010). Dialogue here is not something to be applied in order to facilitate better interpersonal communication, but rather a way of life. It is the natural and ongoing state, in which different perspectives meet and create a new social world. The DOD, thus, views language as the central mechanism of the social construction of reality.

Assuming that the source of thinking and behavior is within the interaction between participants, DOD takes place in face-to-face interactions in group meetings that involve all stakeholders in the organization (employees, managers, directors and even clients). The purpose of these meetings, however, is not just to create a positive atmosphere. The meetings function as intervention programs in which consultants encourage participants to express their views and aspirations. Specifically, the group frameworks have dual purposes. First, they allow open interpersonal interactions in which different perspectives are expressed as a way to produce and reproduce new ideas, images, theories and models of action. Second, they divert existing processes of social construction so as to achieve new personal and collective results. Like AI, DOD devotes itself actively and explicitly to intervention in the processes of the social construction of reality (Gergen, Gergen, and Barrett, 2004).

DOD, then, focuses the change process on when, where and how to promote ongoing successful conversations that legitimize and give voice to an often-hidden variety of perspectives. The logic of these conversations assumes that it is not possible to plan and manage change processes in a separate and preliminary diagnostic stage, as suggested by traditional

OD. Change is brought about mainly by the people themselves in the context of structured and planned conversations on issues related to the organization's future (Bushe, 2010; Cooperrider and Sekerka, 2006).

HOOD vs. Appreciative Inquiry and Dialogic OD

HOOD agrees with AI and DOD in at least three aspects. First, HOOD also draws on social construction, which views individuals as an inseparable part of the social system. Second, like the other two approaches, HOOD sees the perspectives of all participants (not only of managers) as highly relevant and important in organizational change processes. Third, like AI and DOD, HOOD focuses on all three levels: the individual, the group and the organization.

It seems, though, that the theoretical and practical differences between HOOD and AI and DOD are much larger. First, AI and DOD relate to the organization's social reality in harmonious terms. Their theoretical point of departure is that organizations are potentially centers of abilities and positive imagination that can lead to a better future. HOOD, in contrast, views organization as competitive social realties, battlefields of constant struggles for capital and resources. AI and DOD search for organizations' magic and beauty. HOOD, in contrast, seeks to remove the magic covering organizations' social reality to uncover their competitive and struggling nature. AI and DOD largely maintain political neutrality by searching for the positive side of organizations. HOOD, in contrast, explicitly seeks for the political. It searches for ways in which hidden struggles and power relations produce and reproduce organizations' social realities.

Second, AI and DOD are subjective. Their generative power to challenge dominant cultural assumptions, to rethink the obvious, to bring up fresh ideas and perspectives, and to invent new alternatives to social action, is based primarily on the reflective thought of individuals (Gergen, 1978). More specifically, when they deal primarily with language and stories used by individuals to construct social reality, AI and DOD work with the subjectivity of individuals and with the interactions between subjectivities. For them, discursive interactions produce meanings and establish social reality in organizations (Boje, DuRant, Coppedge, Chambers, and Marcillo-Gomez, 2011).

HOOD, on the contrary, distances itself from a pure subjective and interpretive social construction, detached from the material and objective conditions of power and politics. Specifically, HOOD does not see the processes of social construction as the product of subjective or interpersonal relationships but of objective relationships that exist between positions determined by control over kinds of capital. For HOOD, ideas and perspectives are structure-oriented, capital-oriented and position-oriented. Consultees' knowledge of the social reality is never free from structural constraints and opportunities posed by the organization's objective and material aspects.

Third, AI and DOD offer clear intervention practices based on open conversations. One example is the 4-D cycle model that offers a change process in which participants apply changes, evaluate their progress, and engage in new dialogue for AI (Boyd and Bright, 2007, p. 1027; Bushe and Kassam, 2005; Cooperrider and Sekerka, 2006).[1] HOOD, in contrast, does not offer a consulting intervention process itself. It offers sociological and structural critical perspectives for understanding social dynamics in organizations to be conducted by OD's action research and in accordance with OD's philosophy of helping (Schein, 1987).

Nevertheless, it seems that these differences do not necessarily disconnect HOOD and AI and DOD. The open and positive discussions conducted by AI and DOD are valuable for developing consultees' reflexivity to habitus and social structure. HOOD consultants can use AI and DOD conversations and the positive dynamics they produce to explicitly talk about and cope with the organization's socio-political context. That is, they can dedicate the conversations to uncovering and constructively dealing with hidden interests and alliances in the organization, power relations embedded in routine practices and with structures that invisibly control participants' thinking and behavior or leave participants as the only ones responsible for or guilty of the organization's problems.

Fourth, HOOD differs from AI and DOD in its relation to power. AI and DOD do not neglect power, even destructive power. However, they believe that attention to the positive experiences has the potential to eliminate the negative influence of power, to create consensus between individual desires and aspirations and thus reduce the destructive impact of unequal power relations and differences in perspective (Gergen, Gergen, and Barrett, 2004). HOOD is not interested in *bridging* power differences, but in exposing and thus changing the way in which existing power differences take part in the distribution of forms of capital in determining positions and in the construction of the organization's social reality in accordance with capital and positions held by those in power.

To summarize the chapter I would say that HOOD adopts OD's humanistic and democratic values and participative theory and practice that seek to diagnose and solve organizational problems by the participation of many. HOOD also adopts Lewin's systemic approach and field theory, which search for the source of consultees' thinking and behavior in the social context. As stated earlier, however, as opposed to Lewin's field theory, HOOD does not see behavior and social context as relatively stable and separate interacting entities. Instead, for HOOD, behavior and social context are *one* entity enacted by the habitus, constantly produced and reproduced in a competitive social field defined by struggles for the control over capital and position.

Like the individually oriented OD, HOOD encourages OD consultants to adopt therapeutic discourse and practices that focus on consultees' psychological dispositions mainly in order to create effective helping relationships between consultants and consultees and a situation in which responsibility for organizational change stays in the consultees' hands.

HOOD also adopts OD's practices and techniques for self-development and growth, like the T-Group. However, it uses these techniques not for self-development but for the identification and development of participants' reflexivity to habitus and social structure—to the organization's power structure and relations, control over kinds of capital and resources and the consultees' position in this social structure.

Like the systemic approaches of the 1970s and 1980s, HOOD also assumes that individuals and organizations do not operate in social, business, economic or cultural vacuums. However, HOOD tries to overcome the personal-social dichotomy inherent in these approaches, in which the source of consultees' thinking and behavior is the individual *or* the social. Specifically, HOOD does not attempt to change organizations by enlarging and enriching jobs or by re-engineering cultures, or by redefining individuals' mental models. Instead, through face-to-face meetings, HOOD consultants focus on developing consultees' reflexivity to habitus as a starting point for understanding and changing both individual behavior and organizational structures.

Note

1 For more application of the appreciative inquiry, see Hammond (1996).

Bibliography

Anderson, D. L. (2015). *Organization development: The Process of Leading Organizational Change*. Los Angeles, CA: Sage Publications.

Bargal, D. (2011). Kurt Lewin's vision of organizational and social change: The interdependence of theory, research and action/practice. In D. M. Boje, B. Burnes and J. Hassard (Eds.), *The Routledge Companion to Organizational Change*. (pp. 31–45). London and New York: Routledge.

Bargal, D., G. Martin and L. Miriam (1992). Introduction: The heritage of Kurt Lewin. *Journal of Social Issues*, 48(2), 3–13.

Beer, M., R. A. Eisenstat and B. Spector (1990). Why change programs don't produce change. *Harvard Business Review*, 68(6), 4–12.

Boje, D., M. I. DuRant, K. Coppedge, T. Chambers and M. Marcillo-Gomez (2011). Social materiality: A new direction in change management and action research. In D. M. Boje, B. Burnes and J. Hassard (Eds.), *The Routledge Companion to Organizational Change*. (pp. 580–597). London and New York: Routledge.

Boyd, N. M. and D. S. Bright (2007). Appreciative inquiry as a mode of action research for community psychology. *Journal of Community Psychology*, 35(8), 1019–1036.
Bradford, D. L. and W. W. Burke (2005). The future of OD? In D. L. Bradford and W. W. Burke (Eds.), *Reinventing Organization Development: New Approaches to Change in Organizations*. (pp. 195–214). San Francisco, CA: Pfeiffer.
Bradford, D. L. and J. I. Porras (2005). A history view of the future of OD: An interview with Jerry I. Porras. In D. L. Bradford and W. W. Burke (Eds.), *Reinventing Organization Development: New Approaches to Change in Organizations*. (pp. 43–64). San Francisco, CA: Pfeiffer.
Burke, W. W. (1992). *Organization Development: A Process of Learning and Changing*. New York: Addison-Wesley.
Burke, W. W. (2006). Where did OD come from? In J. V. Gallos (Ed.), *Organization Development*. (pp. 13–38). San Francisco, CA: Jossey Bass.
Burke, W. W. (2008). *Organization Change: Theory and Practice*. Thousand Oaks, CA: Sage Publications.
Burke, W. W. (2010). A perspective on the field of organization development and change: The Zeigarnik effect. *The Journal of Applied Behavioral Science*, 47(2), 143–167.
Burnes, B. and D. Bargal (2017). Kurt Lewin: 70 years on. *Journal of Change Management*, 17(2), 91–100.
Burnes, B. and B. Cooke (2012). Review article: The past, present and future of organization development: Taking the long view. *Human Relation*, 65(11), 1395–1429.
Bushe, G. R. (2007). Appreciative inquiry is not (just) about the positive. *OD Practitioner*, 39(4), 30–35.
Bushe, G. R. (2010). Dialogic OD: Turning away from diagnosis. In W. M. Rothwell, J. M. Stavros and R. L. Sullivan (Eds.), *Practicing Organization Development: A Guide for Leading Change*. (third edition). (pp. 617–623). San Francisco, CA: Wiley.
Bushe, G. R. and A. F. Kassam (2005). When is AI transformational? A meta-case analysis. *The Journal of Applied Behavioral Science*, 41(2), 161–181.
Bushe, G. R. and R. J. Marshak (2008). The postmodern turn, in OD. *OD Practitioner*, 40(4), 9–12.
Bushe, G. R. and R. J. Marshak (2009). Revisioning organization development: Diagnostic and dialogic premises and patterns of practice. *The Journal of Applied Behavioral Science*, 45(3), 348–368.
Bushe, G. R. and R. J. Marshak (2013). Dialogic organization development. In B. Jones and M. Brazzel (Eds.), *The NTL Handbook of Organization Development*. (second edition). (pp. 1–4). San Francisco, CA: Pfeiffer.
Coghlan, D. and C. Jacobs (2005). Kurt Lewin on reeducation: Foundations for action research. *The Journal of Applied Behavioral Science*, 41(4), 444–457.
Cooperrider, D. L. and L. E. Sekerka (2006). Toward a theory of positive organizational change. In J. V. Gallos. (Ed.), *Organization Development*. (pp. 223–238). San Francisco, CA: Jossey-Bass.
Cooperrider, D. L. and S. Srivastva (1987). Appreciative inquiry in organizational life. In W. A. Pasmore and R. Woodman. (Eds.), *Research in Organizational Change and Development*. (pp. 129–169). Greenwich, CT: JAI Press.

Costea, B. N. Crump and K. Amiridis (2008). Managerialism, the therapeutic habitus and the self in contemporary organizing. *Human Relation*, 61(5), 661–685.

Cram, F. (2010). AI. *MAI review*, (3), 1–13.

Daft, R. L. and K. E. Weick (1986). Toward a model of organizations as interpretation systems. *Academy of Management Review*, 9(2), 284–295.

Deal, T. E. and A. A. Kennedy (1982). *Corporate Cultures: The Rites and Rituals of Corporate Life*. Harmondsworth: Penguin Books.

Denison, D. R. and G. M. Spreitzer (1991). Organizational culture and organizational development: A competing values approach. *Research in Organizational Change and Development*, 5(1), 1–21.

Fincham, R. and T. Clark (2002). Introduction: The emergence of critical perspective on consulting. In T. Clark and R. Fincham (Eds.), *Critical Consulting New Perspectives on the Management Advice Industry*. (pp. 1–18). Oxford: Blackwell.

Freedman, A. M. (1999). The history of organization development and the NTL institute: What we have learned, forgotten, and rewritten. *The Psychologist-Manager Journal*, 3(2), 125–141.

French, W. L. (1977). Organization development: Objectives, assumptions, and strategies. In H. L. Tosi and W. C. Hammer (Eds.), *Organizational Behavior and Management: A Contingency Approach*. (pp. 488–504). Chicago, IL: St. Clair press.

French, W. L. and C. H. Bell, Jr. (1999). *Organization Development: Behavioral Science Interventions for Organization Improvement*. Norwood, NJ: Prentice Hall.

Friedlander, F. and L. D. Brown (1974). Organization development. *Annual Review of Psychology*, 25(1), 313–341.

Gergen, K. J. (1978). Toward a generative theory. *Journal of Personality and Social Psychology*, 36(11), 1344–1360.

Gergen, K. J., M. M. Gergen and J. F. Barrett (2004). Dialogue: Life and death of the organization. In D. Grant, C. Hardy, C. Oswick, N. Philips and L. Putnam (Eds.), *The Sage Handbook of Organizational Discourse*. (pp. 39–59). Thousand Oaks, CA: Sage Publications. Retrieved from www.swarthmore.edu/sites/default/files/assets/documents/kenneth--gergen/Dialogue_Life_and_Death_of_the_Organization.pdf

Gergen, K. J., S. McNamee and F. Barret (2001). Toward a vocabulary of transformative dialogue. *International Journal of Public Administration*, (24), 697–707.

Greiner, L. E. (1972). Red flags in organization development: Six trends obstructing change. *Business Horizons*, 15(3), 17–24.

Greiner, L. E. and T. G. Cummings (2005). OD: Wanted more alive than dead! In D. L. Bradford and W. W. Burke (Eds.), *Reinventing Organization Development: New Approaches to Change in Organizations*. (pp. 87–112). San Francisco, CA: Pfeiffer.

Hackman, J. R. and G. R. Oldham (1975). Development of job diagnostic survey. *Journal of Applied Psychology*, 60, 159–170.

Hammond, S. A. (1996). *The Thin Book of: Appreciative Inquiry*. Plano, TX: Thin Book.

Katz, D. and R. L. Kahn (1966). *The Social Psychology of Organizations*. New York: Wiley.

Kunda, G. (2009). *Engineering Culture: Control and Commitment in a High-Tech Corporation*. Philadelphia, PA: Temple University Press.

Lewin, K. (1939). Field theory and experiment in social psychology: Concepts and methods. *American Journal of Sociology*, 1, 868–896.

Lewin, K. (1946). Action research and minority problems. *Journal of Social Issues*, 2(4), 34–46.

Lewin, K., R. Lippitt and R. K. White (1939). Patterns of aggressive behavior in experimentally created 'social climates. *The Journal of Social Psychology*, 10(2), 269–299.

Lippitt, G. and R. Lippitt (1978). *The Consulting Process in Action*. San Diego, CA: University Associates.

Marshak, R. J. and G. R. Bushe (2013). An introduction to advances in dialogic organization development. *OD Practitioner*, 45(1), 1–4.

Peters, J. T. and R. H. Waterman (1982). *In Search of Excellence*. New York: Harper and Row.

Rose, N. (1991). Experts of the Soul. *Psychologie und Geschichte*, 91–99. Retrieved from http://journals.zpid.de/index.php/PuG/article/viewFile/103/142

Sanzgiri, J. and J. Z. Gottlieb (1992). Philosophic and pragmatic influences on the practice of organization development, 1950–2000. *Organizational Dynamics*, 21(2), 57–69.

Schein, E. H. (1969). *Process Consultation: Its Role in Organization Development*. Reading, MA: Addison-Wesley.

Schein, E. H. (1987). *Process Consulting: Lessons for Managers and Consultant* (Vol. 2). Reading, MA: Addison-Wesley.

Schein, E. H. (1999). *Process Consultation Revisited: Building the Helping Relationship*. Reading, MA: Addison-Wesley.

Schein, E. H. (2005). Organization development: A wedding of anthropology and Organization therapy. In D. L. Bradford and W. W. Burke (Eds.), *Reinventing Organization Development: New Approaches to Change in Organizations*. (pp. 131–144). San Francisco, CA: Pfeiffer.

Senge, P. M. (1991). *The fifth discipline, the art and practice of the learning organization*. New York: Doubleday Random House.

Shimoni, B. (2017a). A sociological perspective to organization development. *Organizational Dynamics*, 46, 165–170.

Shimoni, B. (2017b). Bringing agency and social structure back into organization development: Toward a practice of habitus consulting. *Journal of Applied Behavioral Science*, 54(2), 208–225.

Trist, E. (1981). The evolution of socio-technical systems. *Issues in the Quality of Working Life: A Series of Occasional Papers*, 2.

3 Taking Bourdieu to Practice

Toward a *Habitus-Oriented* OD (HOOD)

Agent-Structure Theory and the Need for the Concept of Habitus

Habitus is an organizing concept in Bourdieu's theory of action that sociology categorizes as agent-structure theory (Archer, 1988; Bourdieu, 1989; Giddens, 1984) The term "agent" as used in this book signifies individuals or groups; the term "structure" as used here means common language, metaphors and practical knowledge, power relations, social positions and roles. According to agent-structure theory, individuals act in accordance with structures accepted in the social field in which they live. However, they do not simply enact these structures but constantly produce and reproduce them. Social structures and human practice complement each other, and each assumes the presence of the other—they are two sides of the same coin (Giddens, 1984).

For agent-structure theories, the social sciences are not interested in the experiences of the human agent nor in any form of the social. Instead, they focus on social practices that produce and reproduce the social structure that has produced these specific practices (Ritzer, 2000). Anthony Giddens (1984) defines this dialectical process in his structuration theory with the idea of the " 'duality of structure" whereby social structure is not opposed to agents. It (social structure) shapes the practices agents use, but it is also produced by these precise practices. Structures are not external to practices and have no existence of their own but only exist within the practices that agents employ. Research on information systems (IT) uses the duality approach to show how IT systems are both used by people and modified by those same people. Social structures in this research are both embedded in technologies and appropriated by individuals through use (Ellway and Walsham, 2015).

This is how I myself apply the duality approach in my work as an OD consultant. When I meet with consultees, I usually sit on the side and not at the head of the table. Sitting on the side of the table helps me produce helping relationships with my consultees, as defined by OD's "philosophy of helping" (Lippitt and Lippitt, 1978; Ottaway, 1983; Schein, 1987). According to the philosophy of helping, consultants do not act as experts or as managers who provide solutions from the head of the table, but as process consultants who focus on the consultees' reflexivity to self and habitus. Agent-structure theories would view my decision to sit at the side of the table as producing and reproducing the philosophy of helping, which structures my relations with my consultees and defines my role as an OD process consultant. From the agent-structure perspective, the philosophy of helping is not external to the sitting practice—it does not have an independent life, but is the sitting practice itself.

Habitus as the Site in Which Structure and Practice Meet

For agent-structure theory, then, social practices are the site in which social production takes place. It seems, though, that agent-structure theories do not offer sufficient conceptual tools with which to investigate what happens in these sites. We know very little about what really occurs at that meeting point between structures and practices. Bourdieu (1989) responds to this challenge with the concept of habitus. For him, the habitus is an internal, cognitive and bodily social site that embodies structure and practice. In the habitus, structure and practice meet and produce sets of principles that generate people's thoughts and action strategies. As Bourdieu (1990, p. 53) explains,

> [Habitus is] systems of durable, transposable dispositions, structured structures predisposed to function as structuring structures, that is, as principles which generate and organize practices and representations.

Furthermore, as opposed to Bourdieu's theory of action, Giddens's structuration theory does not consider deeply struggles for power and positions and social fields, in which, as Bourdieu shows in this quotation, the habitus develops and functions "as principles which generate and organize practices and representations". Mustafa Emirbayer and Victoria Johnson (2008, pp. 29–30) say that structuration theory "lacks Bourdieu's complementary concerns with fields as spaces of power and struggles and with habitus as generative principles of strategies of action in relation to such fields". Organizational change, for instance, they add, "might be understood to emerge from a pattern of mismatches between members' habitus and their positions in the organization-as-field".

The meeting between social structures and practices, in which habitus develops and acts, then, does not occur in a social vacuum but only in relation to position and power, depending on the resources available in a given social field. According to Abu Tatli, Mustafa Özbilgin, and Mine Karatas-Ozkan (2015),

> Although the structuration theory suggests that structural changes result from changes in repetitive forms of individual and collective acts, Bourdieu has gone further to explain the kind of varied

resources (capital) that individuals [and the individual's habitus] draw on in order to enact their strategies and how their strategies are both negotiated in and shaped by the logic of the field—that is, the social structures—which in turn is altered through enactments of human agency.

Notes on the Epistemological Roots of Bourdieu's Theory of Action

Bourdieu bases his theory of action in large on Ernst Cassirer's (1972) philosophical principles. Cassirer understood social life not only as an empirical reality, objective and real, but as perceived reality and therefore as being continually constructed and reconstructed by human consciousness through a dual process of "identification and discrimination". The identification process, according to Cassirer, involves surrendering to the objective aspects of society, such as myths and beliefs, religion and science, which he defines as the "laws of society". The discrimination process represents disconnection from these specific laws and active construction of new laws.

Bourdieu relies on Cassirer's ideas of identification and discrimination for the development the concept of habitus. He places the habitus at a distance from Claude Levi-Strauss' objective structuralism and from Jean-Paul Sartre's subjective existentialism, which dominated the French intellectual world in the 1950s and 1960s (Swartz, 1997).

Based on his research on kinship relations in North Africa, Bourdieu shows that structural explanations give us only an official picture of social reality and social relations. In reality, according to Bourdieu, people negotiate, argue and compromise with official rules like kinship relations—rules they constantly break in accordance with their own interests and desires. Structural explanations, for Bourdieu, are indifferent to agency and thus do not fully represent the people who are being studied in the structural research. For the concept of habitus, on the contrary, social agents are not passive actors who mechanically act in accordance with an external set of formal rules. Social agents are active producers of meaning using deeply rooted past experiences to improvise action strategies when reacting to constraints and opportunities in the situation they are confronting. Habitus, then, comes from a theory of action that rejects objective views that understand social agents' behavior as a *direct reaction* to external conditions, symbolic and material (Swartz, 2002).

On the other hand, Bourdieu uses the concept of habitus against Sartre's subjectivism and his existentialist theory. Specifically, he argues against seeing social agents' behavior as emerging solely from subjectivity that is not socially affected. Social agents do not act in a way that is free from an external set of formal rules. People do improvise action strategies but they do it under and within structural opportunities and

constraints that they take for granted. "The cultural forms of the practices of everyday life", say Tatli, Özbilgin, and Karatas-Ozkan (2015,
p. 7), "cannot be reduced to 'needs' of the individuals any more than
to the functional imperatives of the collectivity . . . the central concept,
habitus, aims at combining the subjective and the culturally determined
collective elements in these practices".

Bourdieu developed the concept of habitus, then, to understand the
production of social reality in a way that overcomes the personal-social
or subjective-objective dichotomies. For him, social reality is not an
either-or situation (subjective or objective) but a both-and situation we
should understand only by linking practice and structure. In his words,

> Social reality exists, so to speak, twice, in things and in minds, in
> fields and in habitus, outside and inside of agents. And when habitus
> encounters a social world of which it is the product, it finds itself "as
> a fish in water," it does not feel the weight of the water and takes the
> world about itself for granted.
>
> (Wacquant, 1989, p. 43)

A Case Study from My Consulting Experience

In the following, I present a case study from my consulting experiences
with Kimono[1] in order to illustrate what I see as the potential contribution of Bourdieu's theory and concepts to OD theory and practice.
Kimono is an Israeli firm owned by two business groups, Adventure
and Genesis that develops agricultural marine products for export to
Western Europe and Japan. Kimono has 20 direct stakeholders, 9 non-
management employees, 2 managers and 9 board members, of which 4
are owners. Its yearly revenue when I conducted the consulting process
(2008–2015) was about US$1 million.

The Case Study

In a consulting meeting, Omer, the operation manager at Kimono,
described a situation in which an external audit found fault with the
operation department. According to the audit, water delivery pipes were
located inefficiently and wastefully, the drainage holes were not evacu-
ating all the waste generated during production, and the flushing facil-
ity did not meet the required standard. Omer turned to Benny, a senior
employee in the department, and asked for an explanation of the defects
and the reasons for their creation. To his great surprise, he received this
answer from Benny:

> Yes, I knew about these faults before the visit of the external audit
> and I am very glad they got it. Unfortunately, there is no one to talk

to here. The place is not what it used to be, everything is deteriorating. We sat together with all the marine biologists, wrote plans for the development of the farm [in which the agriculture marine are developed]. We were part of the system we loved very much, and then in everything fell apart, thrown into the trash as if it had not existed. In fact, I must admit that I have been waiting for such an external visit for a long time so things will move here. It is good that this audit has come, perhaps because someone will start listening to us!

In our consulting meetings, Omer claimed that he saw Benny's decision not to deal with faults or to report them when they occurred as an "unacceptable" behavior that did not match his expectations, and perhaps even a kind of resistance aimed at him personally. Omer replied to Benny in this way:

I regard your behavior as unacceptable and understand it as irresponsible and as an expression of a low personal commitment to the place that employs you and pays your wage. Elsewhere, I believe, they would treat you harshly and perhaps even ask you to leave. Despite all this, I would rather sit down and try to understand what happened here.

Self as a Source of Thinking and Behavior

Omer did not discipline Benny (for his "irresponsible" behavior and "low personal commitment") but helped him understand his behavior. As he said in our consulting meeting, he did so in order to base his personal relationship with Benny on openness and trust ("that he will always know he can contact me") aimed at giving Benny the necessary conditions to take responsibility for his actions.

Omer's openness and trust, as he explained later, set the conditions necessary for Benny to express his feelings and thoughts freely ("now he feels good"). As I learned from Omer, his decision not to impose sanctions on Benny's "irresponsible" behavior, but to allow him to express his frustrations, personal difficulties and anger, contributed greatly to Benny's positive feelings. It helped Benny understand his behavior, achieve a sense of independence, and improve his personal responsibility—in fact, improve his working abilities and skills. In response, Benny declared that in the future he would personally fix and report any problem rather than waiting for external audits or other factors to do his work for him.

Omer's decision to discuss the situation with Benny using empathetic listening represents a kind of therapeutic discourse and practice that managers often use to change an employee's self, psychological dispositions and behavior. Following Andrew Jefferson (2003, p. 57), I understand therapeutic practices as

> A set of practices and ways of talking about changing a person for the better, more specifically about correcting or addressing a problem or a set of problems. It is not just bodies, or workers that are targeted; it is selves who are subjected to a therapeutic intervention.

I take into account the possibility that Omer's empathetic approach toward Benny continued the helping relationships that I myself used (and still use) in our meetings, yet Omer could adopt other approach I frequently use. He could try to understand Benny's behavior not only by focusing on his self but also on the social conditions in which Benny's behavior took place. Specifically, he could discuss with Benny not only the personal but also the social and structural roots of his (Benny's) decision not to fix and/or report the faults before the external audit. Indeed, as I learned in the following meetings, Benny and the rest of the non-managerial employees worked under very problematic conditions (low wages, shortage of mechanical aids and long hours under the burning sun) accompanied by a deep and often personally insulting involvement of Kimono's owner in the work process. Omer did not consider any of these as possible reasons for Benny's feeling that "there is no one to talk to" but the external audit.

Habitus as a Source of Thinking and Behavior

Habitus functions in at least two levels. It is a "structured structure" since it consists of the objective world and it is a "structuring structure" since it uses the structured structure to generate behavior (Bourdieu, 1989). This is how Omar Lizardo (2004, p. 387) describes these two meanings in his search for the cognitive origins of habitus,

> I distinguish between two major uses that Bourdieu made of the concept of habitus in his work: the habitus as a perceptual and classifying structure, and the habitus as a generative structure of practical action.

Diane Vaughan (2008, p. 71) applies these two major meanings of the habitus in her research into the 1986 space shuttle Challenger accident when she shows how the participants' habitus, directly influenced by "layered structures", generated understandings and behaviors that eventually led to the Challenger crash.

For Bourdieu, then, human behavior is the product of structures. Unlike the idea of individualism that dominates the world of modern organizations, as exemplified by Omer's individually oriented approach,

Bourdieu sees behavior as a creation of social and not only psychological dispositions. As Bob Lingard and Pam Christie (2003, p. 320) argue in their work on education leadership, education leaders' identity and actions should not be understood in psychological terms, what they define as "microprocesses of cognition". Instead, they find that behavior "is a form of internalized social conditioning that constrains thoughts and directs actions". Habitus, Lingard and Christie (2003, p. 320) remind us, is a "sociological, not a psychological concept".

Similarly, I suggest that Omer see Benny's behavior not only as a psychological and private phenomenon (reflecting low motivation and personal resistance) but also as a sociological and collective one. That is, to think of concepts he uses such as commitment, responsibility and involvement, not necessarily as reflecting Benny's psychological dispositions (low personal responsibility and commitment) but rather his social dispositions, or habitus, which embody Kimono's social structure, perceptions, practical knowledge, power relations and collective actions that do not encourage commitment, personal responsibility, reporting and sharing.

Omer cooperated with this direction of thought. He agreed to dedicate our consulting meetings to investigating not only Benny's self and psychological dispositions but also his habitus and the sources of this habitus in Kimono's social structure and the conditions this structure encouraged. (In my consulting work, I use the concept of habitus as a matter of routine). Indeed, in his account of Kimono's social conditions, Omer described an organization saturated with competing interests in which the non-managerial employees are very united against the exclusion they experience in a reality in which their voice is not only unheard but is treated with contempt and condescension.

Furthermore, Omer sketched a situation in which he and the CEO are positioned between Kimono's dominant owner and the marginalized employees who from the lower position of Kimono's hierarchy try to protect their professional field. In this situation, Kimono's owner routinely ignored the CEO and Omer. Based on economic considerations of survival and profit in a very competitive capitalist market, he forced the operation department (very often by approaching employees directly) to make incorrect decisions, as perceived by experts in the marine agriculture field from within and outside Kimono. This ultimately harms Kimono's agricultural production.

In our investigation, then, Omer and I both realized that Benny's decision not to report Omer or to take care of the faults, reflects a shared habitus, or in Bourdieu's words, a "specific habitus" (acquired later in life from groups such as working organizations; Cornelissen, 2016, p. 501) that did not encourage openness and participation, involvement and commitment. Instead, this habitus told non-managerial employees that it is not worthwhile to initiate new things--new initiatives are not welcome, they will not be heard or they will be rejected out of hand.

The Hysteresis Effect

As we explored Kimono's social life more deeply, it became apparent that the avoidance of active participation on the part of the operation department's employees was relatively new. In the recent past, they had taken an active role in developing new ideas and they were equal partners in decision-making processes on diverse issues. At the time of my meeting with Omer, however, they were in a state of confusion that stemmed from the very simple fact that their habitus, their social dispositions, could no longer be realized, a phenomenon Bourdieu defines "hysteresis". In Bourdieu's words hysteresis happens

> [W]hen disparity grows between dispositions in the habitus and the conditions of the field . . . It is a problem of timing. Habitus is too slow a social process to respond to changes in the fields of production, and the social strategies which seek to realize, or reproduce the structure of disposition either fail or become extraordinarily difficult to institute.
> (quoted by Kirschner and Lachicotte, 2001, p. 442)

As Omer described it, then, the increasing involvement of Kimono's owner, who constantly overrode their opinions and actions, put the operation department's employees in a situation in which the habitus that had naturally organized the way they think and act (by way of sharing and taking responsibility) stopped being compatible with the current situation. Benny describes this hysteresis situation in this way:

> The place is not what it used to be, everything is deteriorating. We [the employees in the operation department] sat together with all the marine biologists, wrote plans for the development of the farm. We were part of the system that we love very much, and then in a single moment everything fell apart, thrown into the trash.

Ron Kerr and Sarah Robinson (2009, p. 830) use the hysteresis concept to understand the behavior of Ukrainian workers in a British international corporation working in post-Soviet Ukraine, a period of transition from state socialism to what they define "oligarchic capitalism". Kerr and Robinson find that the Ukrainian workers, who had developed the habitus of dissidents, were able to adapt creatively to practices of domination in the corporation that were analogous to those in which they had engaged in the Soviet Union. Younger Ukrainian employees, on the contrary, who acquired education and entered the labor market after the end of state socialism, "could not" adapt to the corporation's practices of domination, and thus suffered from the hysteresis effect.

Understanding Bourdieu's hysteresis effect encouraged me to keep suggesting Omer to see that Benny's use of the external audit in order to make "things move", as he said, reflects not only low internal commit-ment and motivation but also a determination to accomplish the habitus he acquired at Kimono over the years and that kept affecting the work process. That is, Omer tried to fulfill the habitus that in the past allowed him to take part in decision-making processes, to share his ideas and to influence what was happening at Kimono. As Bourdieu says, "Habitus is too slow a social process to respond to changes in the fields of produc-tion, and the social strategies which seek to realize, or reproduce, the structure of disposition either fail or become extraordinarily difficult to institute".

Capital and Position

Despite the role habitus plays in predisposing thought and behavior, it is impossible to understand the way in which social agents act only in terms of the habitus. Habitus is always connected to power relations deter-mined mainly by the kinds of capital social agents have (Bourdieu, 1989). A principal type of capital is economic capital that, according to Jeffery Everett (2002, pp. 62–63), consists of "nothing more than monetary and material wealth, commodities, and physical resources". A second impor-tant form of capital is cultural capital. The concept of cultural capital shows that for Bourdieu capital is not necessarily material. Knowledge, skill, taste, lifestyle and qualifications are also capital (Bourdieu, 1991). Symbolic capital, however, is apparently the most important in Bourdieu's eyes since it get its power from the other forms of capital. It is a transla-tion of the other forms of capital. Symbolic capital comprises prestige, renown, reputation and personal authority. Other forms of capital are social capital, the ability to use capital of other social agents to promote one's own interests, and human capital, which comprises the knowledge, skills, and expertise that dominate a specific social field.

The control of gallery owners over material resources such as place (buildings), marketing and artistic artifacts, Bourdieu shows (see Neilsen, 1996), are economic capital; artistic skills, such as the language used in the world of art and techniques for evaluating art, are cultural capi-tal. These two kinds of capital are often supplemented by social capital once the gallery owners and art critics surround a supportive group that speaks their language and get legitimation from symbolic capital derived from the prestige they receive in the wake of economic, cultural and social capital. The relative control social agents have of various types of mate-rial and symbolic capital, then, determines the structure of power and the power relations in a given social space. This control gives a dominant position in the field of art and therefore the power to reproduce their habitus and the world of art in terms of this habitus, thereby preserving their position as the dominant elite in the world of art.

In research into institutional entrepreneurship, Julie Battilana (2006, p. 655) claims that understanding institutional entrepreneurship entails an account of social position, the place individuals have in the organization that determines power and control over resources. This is exactly the case with management. Managers' positions have economic capital derived from their control of the organization's material components (budget, buildings). They have cultural capital, including language, significant knowledge and techniques. They have symbolic capital such as prestige that grants them the needed legitimacy to serve as the leaders of the organization and make decisions. They have social capital, derived from the use of other participants' capital to advance their own interests. Specifically, managers, according to Eric Neilsen (1996) in his research into managerial competencies, can identify each other in terms of the way they speak and behave, build on one another's ideas and enlist their own supporters in managerial decisions. Their position allows them to reproduce their habitus as a dominant group in the organization, and to exert a level of control over its social relationships—to change and shape them according to their will.

While a group of managers produces and reproduces the organization's social reality in accordance to their own position and habitus, others, often employees in non-management positions and with less control of capital, largely refer to the existing social reality as taken-for-granted (Bourdieu, 1989). They become the implementers of managements' ideas (Sewell, 1992). This is apparently what happened at Kimono with the owner's active intervention. His strong agency enabled him to produce a new social reality in which, as stated earlier, considerations of economic survival and profit put the operation department's employees in a hysteresis situation. In this situation, they were forced to adapt to the owner's expectations and, in fact, to make decisions that in their eyes made Kimono work in ineffective and inefficient ways (for example, to use inappropriate materials and change agricultural protocols to meet economic demands).

Bourdieu's theory of action, however, suggests that we address social reality in a more varied and complex manner. The fact that powerful agents' worldviews are obtained and distributed by their actual control over significant types of capital does not necessarily create total acceptance of this worldview by the powerless. Social agents have the ability to act creatively in and on the social sphere. This ability, generally acquired by only a few, depending on their access to capital, exists in everyone (Sewel, 1992). Indeed, although a marginalized employee with limited capital, Benny creatively managed to use the external audit's political and cultural capital for his purpose, to change the existing working conditions.

Field

For Bourdieu, habitus (social dispositions) and capital are personal matters belonging to the social agent at the micro level. However, understanding the social agent entails research at the organization's macro level into the social field, the forms of capital and positions that are considered valuable. Social analysis at the micro level requires a clarification at the macro level of the organization as a social field (Maton, 2012).

Fields as Arenas of a Shared Game

Field is a social space in which people play a game according to rules that are different from the rules played by in a near space (Bourdieu, 1991).

> In order for a field to function, there have to be stakes and people prepared to play the game, endowed with the habitus that implies knowledge and recognition of the immanent law of the field, the stakes and so on.
>
> (Bourdieu, 1993, p. 72)

Once adopted, the field's rules, its law and shared stakes largely direct what people can or cannot do. They become an inner structure, natural and durable dispositions (habitus) that predispose people's thinking and behavior (Jenkins, 1992, p. 71).

For Bourdieu (2007, p. 4), then, understanding social agents' behavior requires "first to understand the field with which and against which" that behavior has been formed. Karl Maton (2012, p. 60) says "any attempt to explain practice by using habitus alone is not Bourdieusian". The form and content of social agents' habitus are historically produced and reproduced under specific conditions of a specific social field. Bourdieu (1990, p. 55) says "The habitus is an infinite capacity for generating products—thoughts, perceptions, expressions and actions— whose limits are set by the historically and socially situated conditions of its production". The way in which Bourdieu applies his theoretical work to the examination of the world of art can help also here. According to Bourdieu, anyone can enter the field of art, but only a narrow elite (art critics, consumers, galleries, and of course the artists themselves) can appreciate what is there. Only the elite knows the rules of the game. This familiarity emerges from the control of practical knowledge that is beyond the formal knowledge that appears in manuals dealing with art. This knowledge is the basis of the elite's habitus. Understanding the elite requires first understanding the field of art, the informal knowledge or the social structure that generate the habitus of the elite, and its members' thinking and behavior (Neilsen, 1996).

Fields as Arenas of Competition and Struggle

Although fields represent a group with common rules, with a shared interest and habitus, group members are always in competition over similar sets of capitals; their "behavior is organized around that competition" (Dobbin, 2008, p. 55). In *On Television and Journalism*, Bourdieu (1998) provides the following definition for the field as arenas of competition:

> A field is a structured social space, a field of forces, a force field. It contains people who dominate and people who are dominated. Constant, permanent relationships of inequality operate inside this space, which at the same time becomes a space in which the various actors struggle for the transformation or preservation of the field. All the individuals in this universe bring to the competition all the (relative) power at their disposal. It is this power that defines their position in the field and, as a result, their strategies.
>
> (Quoted by Lingard and Christie, 2003, p. 322)

Bourdieu's view of social fields as competitive offers another way to understand Benny's behavior. This way also does not see Benny's decision to wait for external audit as an expression of psychological dispositions, his low motivation and commitment, as Omer suggested. Instead, it sees Benny's behavior a result of his habitus, enacted by a dominated employee who is desperately struggling to improve his working conditions in a competitive social field—a field wherein his employers constantly deny his right to take an active role in work processes such as the initiation of new ideas and participation in decision-making.

The struggles that Bourdieu is interested in, those he claims must be taken into account if one wants to understand the way people think and behave, then, are not between emotions and other psychological dispositions, nor they are between consciousness reflecting the subjectivity of actors. Rather, these struggles are between objective positions (roles and organizational and non-organizational units) who are constantly in competition for capital and resources and for influential positions in and out of the organization's social field. As Bourdieu (Wacquant, 1989, p. 39) says, a field is

> [A] network, or a configuration, of objective relations between positions objectively defined, in their existence and in the determinations they impose upon their occupants, agents or institutions, by the present and potential situation (situs) in the structure of the distribution of species of power (or capital) whose possession commands access to the specific profits that are at stake in the field.

Understanding the interaction between Omer and Benny, then, also entails an account of the objective relations between the two, their unequal power relations and different positions at Kimono. Put another way, a reduction of Omer and Benny's interaction to the level of interpersonal relations, as Omer did when he defined Benny's behavior as resistance to him personally, does not explain fully what happened between the two. To understand that, one should consider not only the subjective but also the objective aspects of their interaction, especially the different place the two have in Kimono's formal hierarchy—the differences in capitals and positions. Specifically, omitting the objective aspect of Omer and Benny's interaction would ignore the fact that this interaction was between an employee, whose authority and other ways of expression were taken from him, and a manager, who has legitimate power to maintain or change Benny's working conditions. For Bourdieu, as Anna Leander (2001, p. 348) stresses in her review of his (Bourdieu's) perspective on the economic field, "structure has effects independently of the interaction of agents and even independently of their consciousness".

Furthermore, Bourdieu (1993, p. 82) reminds us that social interactions never take place in a social vacuum. That is, social interactions are not

> an empire within an empire . . . what happens between two persons, between a house owner and her servant, between two colleagues or between a French speaker and a German speaker is always controlled by the objective relations *between the two groups* speaking these languages . . . when a German-speaking Swiss talks to a French-speaking Swiss, it is German Switzerland and Francophone Switzerland that are talking.
>
> (Italics mine)

Following Bourdieu's understanding of social interactions, I claim, then, that focusing merely on the subjective negotiation between Omer and Benny would have ignored not only the objective aspect (position and capitals) between the two, but also the wider interactions within which this negotiation took place (Emirbayer and Johnson, 2008). Specifically, considering only the interaction between the two (subjective and objective) would not recognize that Benny's behavior largely reflected the relationship between excluded employees and excluding management. In the interaction between Benny and Omer, then, marginalized employees and marginalizing management were actually those who "spoke" to each other and not only Benny and Omer (Bourdieu and Wacquant, 1992).

Strategies, Field's Doxa and reflexivity

As stated earlier, the position social agents occupy in the social field produces their habitus and behavior. However, as Benny shows in his use of the external audit, social agents are not "cultural dopes" (Sewell, 1992, p. 15). They use creative strategies to gain control over capital and improve their position. As Özbilgin, Tatli, and Queen (2005, p. 864) say,

> The fact that the meaning and volume of capital and dispositions held by the individuals are dependent on the principles of habitus and field does not mean that they are devoid of voluntary action. Individuals use strategies to transform, allocate, and distribute their volume of capital among different forms, which, in turn, determine the boundaries of their agency—that is, the sphere of their active action and voluntarism—within the habitus and field they are acting in.

Strategy "is the habitus in action", Lingard and Christie (2003, p. 322) say. It is both the product of the social structure as embedded in the social agent's dispositions, habitus and the producer of the field's social structure, its power relations, organizing metaphors and practical knowledge. Bourdieu offers at least three strategies that constantly struggle to shape the field's social structure: conservation, succession and subversion. The *conservation* strategy is used by those who hold dominant positions in the field and are interested in maintaining the existing situation. The *succession* strategy comes from those who seek to gain entry into dominant positions in the field. The *subversion* strategy comes from those in lower positions with small amounts of capital or from those who wish to undermine the existing social reality and redefine the criteria upon which something becomes real (for example, certain knowledge or behaviors) (Chopra, 2003). The subversion strategy challenges the legitimacy of powerful agents who hold dominant positions in the field and define the field's cultural capital.

Bourdieu (1993, p. 73) calls the subversive strategy also "heterodoxy" (opposite to orthodoxy) or "heresy" that works to disrupt the accepted "doxa". Doxa is defined as the social field's specific-habitus, its unspoken understandings. It comprises "assumptions that go without saying and which determine the limits of the doable and the thinkable" (Maton, 2012, p. 58). "It is a pre-reflexive intuitive knowledge shaped by experience" (Deer, 2012, p. 114), or the "shared beliefs and taken-for-granted assumptions" (Bourdieu, 2000, quoted by Sieweke, 2014) that define what is valuable in a given social field. From this perspective, I see Benny's use of the external audit as a heresy strategy that challenged the operation department's doxa. According to this doxa, employees should show total commitment and responsibility and a high innovative and productive behavior (for instance, independently fix problems), regardless of working conditions and other social issues such as asymmetric power structure and relations, and control over capitals and positions.

Benny's use of the external audit to challenge the existing doxa and make his way out of the bottom of Kimono's social structure put in question one of the most important theoretical assumptions of this book and of my consulting intervention at Kimono. According to this assumption, social agents' practices are habitus-driven and thus pre-reflexive, not intentional, unconscious or rational. Still, Benny apparently knew exactly what he was doing. His call for the external audit for help was intentional, reflexive and rational. As he said, "I have to admit that I have long been waiting for such an external audit so that things will move here".

Indeed, critics question Bourdieu's assertion that habitus-driven behaviors and strategies are unconscious and without intention. Richard Jenkins (2002, p. 93), for example, stresses that Bourdieu reduces conscious activity to body activity while Jeffery Alexander (1995, p. 144; quoted by Atkinson, 2010, p. 11), asserts that by removing reflexivity and intentionality from social life, Bourdieu "ignore[s] the complexities and subjectivities that the category 'self' implies".

A careful reading of Bourdieu, however, shows that he has never denied consciousness and rational action. Rational action, for him, is not common but appears in times of crisis (Deer, 2012). I see the hysteresis effect discussed here, in which Benny's habitus fails to fit into the new situation, as an expression of a time of crisis. At such times, in which Benny's social dispositions such as sharing and participation could no longer be realized, I would claim that Benny intentionally took advantage of the external audit capital.

Symbolic Violence

Benny's decision not to deal with the faults but wait for the external audit, then, largely reflects a heresy strategy reflexively exercised by a powerless employee in an attempt to change the operation department's accepted doxa and the working conditions this doxa encourages. Applying heresy strategies, however, is only part of the story. Very often, the heresy strategy pushes powerful agents to protect practically and discursively the existing situation in which the ruling position is a natural part of the doxa, the taken-for-granted social reality. In Bourdieu's (1993, p. 73) words,

> Heresy, heterodoxy, functioning as a critical break with doxa (and often associated with crisis), is what brings the dominant agents out of their silence and forces them to produce the defensive discourse of orthodoxy, the right-thinking, right-wing thought that is aimed at restoring the equivalent of silent assent to doxa.

One way dominant agents use to protect the doxa is "symbolic violence", an implicit, constant and routine strategy that those in power use to maintain and expand the doxa and the existing power structures it supports. This is how Bourdieu (1998) defines symbolic violence: "Symbolic violence is violence wielded with tacit complicity between its victims and its agents, insofar as both remain unconscious of submitting to or wielding it" (p. 17). In fact, symbolic violence does what police and political forces do, but only more effectively. This is because symbolic violence is tacit. It lies beyond, or below, the control of consciousness and personal will, and the power it exercises is usually experienced as something good. Unlike purposeful, hierarchical and political power, symbolic violence is wielded more easily on the people on whom it is employed, and very often even injects a belief that it benefits them, even though at the end it reproduces a social reality that is totally against their interests (Everett, 2002).

I claim that Omer's empathetic approach, which focused on 'improving' Benny's self, represents pure symbolic violence. It is *violent* since like any other traditional force it forced Benny to move from point A to point B against his original will. Benny sought to change social conditions but eventually found himself changing his communication skills and other psychological dispositions such as commitment and responsibility. Specifically, Benny tried to use the external audit to change the structural conditions in which his habitus was no longer relevant and to move from his marginalized position to a more participative position. Instead, through the supportive meetings with Omer, he moved from being an 'unconcerned' employee (point A) to a better employee who effectively communicates his needs (point B). As shown, Benny acknowledged that he behaved inappropriately and promised to fix and report any problem on time, to behave in a more responsible way that would reflect a greater commitment to Kimono.

Omer's empowering and supportive approach is *symbolic* because it helped him (Omer) enforce his will on Benny and undermine his interests in an invisible way, without Benny noticing it. What enabled this invisibility, and thus Benny's acceptance of participation in a self-development process, I claim, was the role of the mentor, counselor, or natural pedagogue Omer played. As Pierre Bourdieu and Jean-Claude Passeron (1977, p. 5) argue, all pedagogic actions are possibly symbolic violence since they are "the imposition of a cultural arbitrary by an arbitrary power" (quoted by Deetz, 1992, p. 28). That is, although well-intentioned, pedagogic actions impose meanings on people in a legitimate way derived from the concealed exercise of power relations. Put another way, taking the role of the pedagogue, a neutral and impartial professional who seeks his employee's well-being, allowed Omer to hide the asymmetric power relations that served him to make Benny involved in self-improvement rather than in improving his working conditions, as he first wanted to.

Social Equilibrium and Relational Theory of Practice

Both Benny's heresy strategy and Omer's symbolic violence largely reflect the idea of social equilibrium Bourdieu adopted from Cassirer (1972).

According to Cassirer, fields are social spaces whose social equilibrium is determined by dynamic forces operated by social agents who constantly do everything they can to accumulate kinds of capital and improve their position in the field *in relation* to the capitals they themselves and others already have. In Cassirer's (1972, p. 279) words: "If there is an equipoise in human culture it can only be described as a dynamic, not as a static equilibrium; it is the result of a struggle between opposing forces". Following Cassirer, Bourdieu claims that social equilibrium is the result of struggles in the social field, of actions and counter-actions. Social equilibrium is not a static but a dynamic situation continually produced and reproduced on the move by struggle and competition between opposing forces. Benny's heresy strategy (in which he tried to change the existing social conditions) and Omer's symbolic violence (in which he related indirectly to those specific social conditions as taken-for-granted) are opposing processes that constitute the operation department's social equilibrium. In other words, Benny and Omer's interaction represents a "more than simply [different] worldview in the classical sociological sense" (Dobbin, 2008, p. 58). Instead, their interaction represents the operation department's social equilibrium characterized by constant struggle and competition over capitals and positions, negotiated and formed by the habitus of a marginalized employee and an authoritative manager, operating in Kimono's social field.

Considering the interaction between Omer and Benny in terms of social equilibrium produced through struggles and competition matches with Bourdieu's *relational* thinking (Vandenberghe, 1999). Bourdieu, says David Swartz (1997), criticizes "substantialism" and "realism". He sees the two ideas as an "obstacle to developing genuine scientific knowledge of the social world" since they encourage an epistemology that "recognizes", as Bourdieu says, "no other reality than that which is directly given to the intuition of ordinary experience" (quoted by Swartz, 1997, p. 61). Relational thinking, on the other hand, "identifies the real not with substance but with relationships" (Swartz, 1997, pp. 61–62). "In Bourdieu's analysis", according to Cynthia Forson, Mustafa Özbilgin, Mustafa Bilgehan Ozturk, and Ahu Tatli (2014, p. 64), "key concepts such as habitus, field, capitals and strategies, work together to generate the social reality as he sets out". "Bourdieu's great power", says Frank Dobbin (2008, p. 53), "comes from its integration of a theory of the individual (habitus), a theory of social structure (the field), and a theory of power relations (the various forms of capital)".

Writers stress that American organizational researchers often detach Bourdieu's key concepts from the deep logic of his relational thinking (Dobbin, 2008). This partial use of Bourdieu's concepts, they say, impoverish organizational research (Emirbayer and Johnson, 2008; Golsorkhi, Leca, Lounsbury, and Ramirez, 2009)—it does not fully apply Bourdieu's theory, even if it uses some of its concepts (Sieweke, 2014). Bourdieu understands all his major concepts as connected relationally. "Strictly speaking", says Swartz (2008, p. 47), "Bourdieu does not offer a theory of fields, a theory of capital, or a theory of habitus, as stand-alone conceptual perspectives".

For organizational research and especially for change management research and practice like OD, the relational approach is highly significant. One cannot understand Benny's heresy strategy without understanding Kimono's doxa with its marginalizing social structure and asymmetric power relations and without considering his degraded position and hysteresis effect after losing lot of his kinds of capital. As Everett (2002, p. 57) rightly claims, applying a relational theory "[M]eans seeing the organization as embedded in a 'field' of relations, one wherein actors constantly struggle to accumulate 'capital,' that fleeting form of power whose value is always and only ever field specific".

Some organizational researchers, however, do use Bourdieu's theory of practice in a relational form. Vaughan (2008) does so in her study on the Challenger crash in which she refers to the structural constraints from inside and outside the field that shaped the specific habitus of the experts and the management. Forson, Özbilgin, Ozturk, and Tatli (2014, p. 66) use Bourdieu's concepts in a complementary way by linking the concepts of field, habitus, capitals and strategies to provide "holistic and interconnected" frameworks which combine macro, meso and micro levels of entrepreneurs of small business (ESB). As they say, the relational approach enabled them to represent together "explanations of interactions and interrelationships between the levels of individual and society" (p. 66).

Being a HOOD consultant with a relational perspective, then, means thinking and working in relational terms. That is, we must explicitly consider the relational nature of the organization's social reality in which negotiations between objective positions, defined and generated by struggles over capitals and thus power, produce and reproduce social structures and personal dispositions. Practically, it means developing consultees' *reflexivity* to habitus and social structure and to the social positions and conditions produced by this structure. Working in relational terms, then, means understanding that in the social world, as Bourdieu keeps saying, "[T]he real is relational: what exist in the social world are relations, not interactions between agents or intersubjective ties between individuals, but objective relations, which exist independently of individual consciousness" (Wacquant, 1989, p. 39).

Note

1 All names (people and the organizations) are pseudonyms. All quotations from Kimono's members translated from Hebrew.

Bibliography

Alexander, J. C. (1995). *Fin de Siècle Social Theory: Relativism, Reduction, and the Problem of Reason*. New York: Verso.

Archer, M. S. (1988). *Culture and Agency: The Place of Culture in Social Theory.* London: Cambridge University Press.

Atkinson, W. (2010). Phenomenological additions to the Bourdieusian toolbox: Two problems for Bourdieu, two solutions from Schutz. *Sociological Theory,* 28(1), 1–19.

Battilana, J. (2006). Agency and institutions: The enabling role of individuals' social position. *Organization,* 13(5), 653–676.

Bourdieu, P. (1977). *Outline of a Theory of Practice.* Cambridge, MA: Cambridge University Press.

Bourdieu, P. (1989). Social space and symbolic power. *Sociological Theory,* 7(1), 14–25.

Bourdieu, P. (1990). *The Logic of Practice.* (Translated: R. Nice). Stanford, CA: Stanford University Press.

Bourdieu, P. (1991). *Language and Symbolic Power.* Cambridge, MA: Polity Press.

Bourdieu, P. (1993). *Sociology in Question.* London: Sage Publication.

Bourdieu, P. (1998). *On Television and Journalism.* (Translated: Priscilla Parkhurst and Ferguson). London: Pluto.

Bourdieu, P. (2000). *Pascalian Meditations.* Stanford, CA: Stanford University Press.

Bourdieu, P. (2007). *Sketch for a Self-analysis.* Cambridge, England: Polity Press.

Bourdieu, P. and Passeron, J. C. (1977). *Reproduction in Education, Society and Culture.* London: Sage Publications.

Bourdieu, P. and Wacquant, L. (1992). *An Invitation to Reflexive Sociology.* Chicago, IL and London: University of Chicago Press.

Cassirer, E. (1972). *An Essay on Man* (1944). New Haven/London: Yale University Press.

Chopra, R. (2003). Neoliberalism as doxa: Bourdieu's theory of the state and the contemporary Indian discourse on globalization and liberalization. *Cultural Studies,* 17(3–4), 419–444.

Cornelissen, S. (2016). Turning distaste into taste: Context-specific habitus and the practical congruity of culture. *Theory and Society,* 45(6), 501–529.

Deer, C. (2012). Doxa. In *Pierre Bourdieu: Key Concepts.* (second edition). (pp. 48–64). London and New York: Routledge.

Deetz, S. A. (1992). *Democracy in an Age of Corporate Colonization.* Albany, NY: State University of New York Press.

Dobbin, F. (2008). The poverty of organizational theory: Comment on Bourdieu and organizational analysis. *Theory and Society,* 37, 53–63.

Ellway, B. P. and G. Walsham (2015). A doxa-informed practice analysis: Reflexivity and representations, technology and action. *Information Systems Journal,* 25(2), 133–160.

Emirbayer, M. and V. Johnson (2008). Bourdieu and organizational analysis. *Theory and Society,* 37(1), 1–44.

Everett, J. (2002). Organizational research and the praxeology of Pierre Bourdieu. *Organizational Research Methods,* 5(1), 56–80.

Forson, C., M. Özbilgin, M. B. Ozturk and A. Tatli (2014). Multi-level approaches to entrepreneurship and small business research: Transcending dichotomies with Bourdieu. In E. Chell and M. Karatas-Ozkan (Eds.), *Handbook of*

Research on Small Business and Entrepreneurship. (pp. 54–69). Cheltenham: Edward Elgar Publishing.

Giddens, A. (1984). *The Constitution of Society: Outline of the Theory of Structuration.* Berkeley, CA: University of California Press.

Golsorkhi, D., B. Leca, M. Lounsbury and C. Ramirez (2009). Analyzing, accounting for and unmasking domination: On our role as scholars of practice, practitioners of social science and public intellectuals. *Organization*, 16(6), 779–797.

Jefferson, A. M. (2003). Therapeutic discipline? Reflections on the penetration of sites of control by therapeutic discourse. *Critical Practice Studies*, 5(1), 55–73.

Jenkins, R. (1992). *Pierre Bourdieu.* London and New York: Routledge.

Kerr, R. and S. Robinson (2009). The hysteresis effect as creative adaption of the habitus: Dissent and transition to the 'corporate' in post-soviet Ukraine. *Organization*, 16(6), 829–853.

Kirschner, S. R. and W. S. Lachicotte (2001). Managing managed care: Habitus, hysteresis and the end (s) of psychotherapy. *Culture, Medicine and Psychiatry*, 25(4), 441–456.

Leander, A. (2001). Review essay: Pierre Bourdieu on economics. *Review of International Political Economy*, 8(2), 344–353

Lingard, B. and P. Christie (2003). Leading theory: Bourdieu and the field of educational leadership. An introduction and overview to this special issue. *Leadership in Education*, 6(4), 317–333.

Lippitt, G. and R. Lippitt (1978). *The Consulting Process in Action.* San Diego, CA: University Associates.

Lizardo, O. (2004). The cognitive origins of Bourdieu's habitus. *Journal of the Theory of Social Behavior*, 34(4), 375–401.

Maton, K. (2012). Habitus. In *Pierre Bourdieu: Key Concepts* (second addition). (pp. 48–64). London and New York: Routledge.

Neilsen, E. H. (1996). Modernism, postmodernism and managerial competencies: A multidiscourse reading. In D. M. Boje, R. P. Gephart Jr. and T. J. Thatchenkery (Eds.), *Postmodern Management* and *Organization Theory.* (pp. 266–292). Thousand Oaks, CA: Sage Publications.

Ottaway, R. N. (1983). The change agent: A taxonomy in relation to the change process. *Human Relations*, 36(4), 361–392.

Özbilgin, M., A. Tatli and M. Queen (2005). Book review essay: Understanding Bourdieu's contribution to organization and management studies, [Review of Outline of Theory of Practice]. The logic of practice; practical reason: On the theory of action; An invitation to reflexive sociology. *The Academy of Management Review*, 30(4), 855–869.

Ritzer, G. (2000). *Modern Sociological Theory.* New York: McGraw-Hill Education.

Schein, E. H. (1987). *Process Consultation: Lessons for Managers and Consultants.* (Vol. 2). Reading, MA: Addison-Wesley.

Sewell, Jr. W. H. (1992). A theory of structure: Duality, agency, and transformation. *American Journal of Sociology*, 98(1), 1–29.

Sieweke, J. (2014). Pierre Bourdieu in management and organization studies: A citation context analysis and discussion of contributions. *Scandinavian Journal of Management*, 30(4), 532–543.

Swartz, D. L. (1997). *Culture and Power: The Sociology of Pierre Bourdieu.* Chicago, IL and London: University of Chicago Press.

Swartz, D. L. (2002). The sociology of habit: The perspective of Pierre Bourdieu. *The Occupational Therapy Journal of Research*, 22, 61s-69s.

Swartz, D. L. (2008). Bringing Bourdieu's master concepts into organizational analysis. *Theory and Society*, 37(1), 45–52.

Tatli, A., M. Özbilgin and M. Karatas-Ozkan (2015). Introduction: Management and organization studies meet Pierre Bourdieu. In A. Tatli, M. Özbilgin and M. Karatas-Ozkan (Eds.), *Pierre Bourdieu, Organization, and Management.* (pp. 1–16). London and New York: Routledge.

Vandenberghe, F. (1999). "The Real is Relational": An epistemological analysis of Pierre Bourdieu's generative structuralism. *Sociological Theory*, 17(1), 32–67.

Vaughan, D. (2008). Bourdieu and organizations: The empirical challenge. *Theory and Society*, 37(1), 65–81.

Wacquant, L. J. (1989). Towards a reflexive sociology: A workshop with Pierre Bourdieu. *Sociological Theory*, 1, 26–63.

4 Organization Development and Society

OD needs to re-engage with the big questions concerning society and organizations and, in return, this engagement has the power to motivate the practitioner and academic wings of OD to reunite.

—(Burnes and Cooke, 2012, p. 1417)

Individualism, Blame and Control

Omer's symbolic violence, in which he implicitly and supportively puts the responsibility for Benny's behavior solely on Benny's shoulders, apparently did not correspond *only* with the empowering language and practice of OD that I used in our consulting meeting. Omer's behavior, I claim, also reflects an individualistic orientation rooted in Western social structure and modern organizations like Kimono. In this structure, engrained in the enlightenment's rational thought, the individual is an autonomic psychological subject, entitled to self-expression and self-actualization (De Vos, 2010; Gergen and Thatchenkery, 1996; Shimoni, 2017).

Individualism, says Eva Illouz (2008, p. 9), is a good example of a philosophy that a vast range of institutions hold. Significant examples for the individualistic philosophy are in fields such as education, law and labor (Gergen, Gergen, and Barrett, 2004). Managers and organizations in the labor market, which is the social context of this book, use psychological discourse and practices in order to define modern organizations as sites of self-expression and realization (Rose, 1991). Exchanges such as *"what is wrong with me?" "Just focus and everything will go well; it is only a question of how much effort you are willing to invest"* reflect a belief in which the individual is the main source of meanings, values and practical norms, and thus fully responsible for his or her behavior and needs, for better or worse (Gergen, Gergen, and Barrett, 2004).

Self-responsibility, then, as enacted by employees' social dispositions, or habitus, became a significant component of modern organizations. This habitus, I would argue, blames the individual for failures at both the individual and the organizational levels, and in a process of *self-blaming*, the individual voluntarily takes full responsibility for problems. According to Stephen Mick (1973), quoted by Chauvière and Mick (2013, p. 139), very often employees

> faced with constant corporate restructuring . . . taking out on one's self the personal blame for failures that are actually organizationally—or managerially—derived . . . [I]individuals tend to blame themselves for problems that they experience but that are socially or economically derived.

The blaming and self-blaming effect very often puts the self at the center of organizational change processes; managers expect employees to continually 'work' on themselves and improve their personal skills and abilities in order to prevent future problems. This is exactly what Omer and Benny's interaction shows. Their interaction started when Omer blamed Benny for being the only one responsible for his decision not to fix or report the problems exposed by the external audit and ended with Omer's effort to fix Benny's behavior. In organizations, according to Bogdan Costea, Norman Crump, and Costas Amiridis (2008, p. 672) the position of authority is placed in "a new form of individualism":

> It creates a self that considers itself more than just self, as something deeper, more natural and authentic than the ordinary self-does. Self as a self that has to work on itself to enrich and find itself in the process of dealing with its problems.

Omer's attempt to fix Benny's self using positive language seems to represent a process in which the individual self becomes an apparatus in the service of "soft capitalism" (Costea, Crump, and Amiridis, 2008). The word "soft", suggest Costea, Crump, and Amiridis (2008, p. 672), refers to the "expansion and intensification of demands on the self to become ever more involved in work with its whole subjectivity". That is, this self, as the interaction between Omer and Benny shows, has become the site in which regulation of the work process happens. As Tomas Klikauer (2015, p. 1008) says, in the capitalist modern organization the self "does not exist 'for-itself', it has a goal, a function—it serves control and surveillance". Indeed, by using active and empathetic listening Omer gently helped Benny build a 'better' self, one that he can control and regulate so it fits his (Omer's) expectations (Omer: *Elsewhere, I believe, they would treat you harshly . . . I would rather sit down and try to understand what happened here.* Benny: *[I]n the future, I will . . . act immediately and independently to correct and/or report deficiencies*).

Managerialism

I would claim that Omer's symbolic violence, through which he made Benny change his behavior and believe in his (Omer's) perspective, represents a managerialist approach (Boje, 2012; Clegg, 2014). Management as understood in this book aims to do things through non-managers, individuals and groups while considering their needs and perspectives. Managerialism, rather, aims to do things in a way that considers managers' needs and perspectives first.

The managerialist approach, says Stanley Deetz (1992, p. 229), has been defined as the "desire for control, a will to power . . . which makes managerial success a means to everyone's ends". It focuses first on the organizational manager, on his/herself and on economic goals such as efficiency, effectiveness and profitability (Mills, Simmons, and Mills, 2010). Actually, managerialism is a pure ideology or philosophy that supports the interests of a small part of society as if it were the universal interest (Klikauer, 2013). William Roy (1999) argues that the corporate governance regime, explicitly searching for efficiency and public good, serves to further economic capital purposes and goals as defined by the regime. Specifically, the managerialist approach grants the corporate governance regime discourse and practices aiming to construct the individual and the social context in a way that can potentially enhance productivity. It is "a set of discursive moves that interpellates a particular type of subject and produces a particular world" (Deetz, 1992, p. 222). As an instrument of governance, as the interaction of Benny and Omer shows, managerialism has developed the practices needed to subordinate the individual's self to considerations of control and profit defined by managers.

Managerialism developed as part of the accelerated capitalism at the end of the last century from the need of an emerging managerial group to control workers and develop organizations that are more efficient. To quote Robert Locke and J.C. Spender (2011, p. x), managerialism is comprised of "business managers [that] have come to view themselves as a professional caste". According to Eva Illouz (2008, pp. 64–65),

> From the increasing number of workers and the need to discipline them emerged a managerial class who were neither owners nor workers and who viewed themselves as vested with the social mission of increasing production by managing workers.

The managerial class, then, is a product of capitalism, of a free market that encourages values of productivity and efficiency. In fact, managerialism and capitalism are two sides of the same coin. Both translate economic and social problems into managerial issues to be solved by effective management while social, ethical and political dimensions are considered secondary. Both generate social and economic inequality that works against democracy in the workplace and justifies the domination of a group with institutionalized power (Klikauer, 2013). Both produce competition and inequality. Both assume that there is no democratic solution to problems but rather a management solution (Glover, 2013). Social problems for both can be managed just like technical problems (Baldry and Barnes, 2012; Fleming and Sturdy, 2009).

Claiming that they possess the needed knowledge to raise productivity in corporations and societies, managerialism and capitalism diffuse their competitive and for-profit management discourse and practices to all sectors of society. Instances are the government, philanthropy and the education system (Shimoni, forthcoming). As Mats Alvesson and André Spicer (2016) show, these sectors very often voluntarily surrender their traditional values and practices to managerialism:

> There are many examples of professionals surrendering their autonomy in the face of managerial change agendas. It has happened in health care as management systems have been imported from automobile manufacturing to control the workflow of doctors. It has happened in the law as traditional partnerships have become corporations. Now even priests are being sent on management training courses in business schools.
>
> (p. 29)

By establishing its power and control, aimed mainly to achieve profitability and effectiveness, managerialism enacts a non-ethical behavior that eliminates resistance (Lynch, 2014; Mueller and Carter, 2007). See Omer's symbolic violence and Benny's *quick adoption* of his (Omer's) expectations. Indeed, facing this non-ethical behavior in the case of Omer and Benny put me in a dilemma: should I help Omer overcome Benny's resistance (by developing Omer's communication skills, for example) and ignore Benny's attempts to work in a more democratic and sharing situation, thus voluntarily enacting a non-ethical managerialist consulting approach? Alternatively, should I stick to OD's humanistic and democratic values and its helping philosophy and first help Omer 'listen' to Benny and explore what his behavior really says? This is how Bernard Burnes and Bill Cooke (2012, pp. 1416–1417) describe the historical development of this dilemma:

> In the 1960s, OD continued to address fundamental questions about the nature of society and organizations . . . [s]ince then, OD has narrowed its ambitions to such an extent that it has been in danger of sacrificing 'the goals of the individuals within the organization' (French and Bell, 1973, p. xvi) in order to 'enable organizations to be

effective' (Cummings, 2005, p. 25). This has led to accusations, especially from critical management theorists, that it is merely a vehicle for managerialist co-optation.

OD's Humanistic Values

Before I explore this dilemma further, let me first briefly sketch OD's humanistic values that have been integral part of the field from its beginning (Piotrowski and Armstrong, 2004). For OD founders, values provide the deep logic for applying and understanding OD interventions (Anderson, 2015; Burke, 1992, 2008; Schein, 1990). "Organization development", say Allan Church, Janine Waclawski, and Wes Seigel (1996, p. 49), "is a field based on values—promoting positive humanistically oriented large-systems change in organizations—plain and simple".

Kurt Lewin's concerns with the devastating power of the Nazi autocracy and thus his interest in participative democracy comprise the conceptual bases of OD's organizing value system. Specifically, although the name OD was not familiar in Lewin's time,[1] his personal history in Nazi Germany, in which he lost part of his family, and his experience as an immigrant and part of a minority group, constitute OD's humanistic and democratic value system. Lewin says that

> Democracy is opposed to both autocracy and laissez-faire. It includes long-range planning by the group on the basis of self-responsibility; it recognizes the importance of leadership, but this leadership remains responsible to the group as a whole and does not interfere with the basic equality of rights for every member. The safeguard of this equality of status is the emphasis on reason and fairness rather than personal willfulness. The right to influence group policy must have as its counterpart the willingness to accept majority decisions.
>
> (Quoted by Burnes and Bargal, 2017, p. 95)

It seems that one of the most significant sites in which OD's humanistic and democratic values developed were the "Sensitivity Training Groups" (Burke, 1992, p. 179) called later on T-Groups. The T-Groups, claim Burnes and Cooke (2012, p. 1400), "[S]tressed personal growth, emotional expression, and the need to challenge bureaucracy and promote democratic participation, which matched the hippy, antiauthoritarian spirit of the age as epitomized by the civil rights and peace movements". Newton, Margulies, and Anthony Raia (1988; quoted by Anderson, 2015, p. 41), say that OD "is value-based and more importantly its core values provide the guiding light for both the OD process and its technology. The very identity of the field is reflected in the existence and application of the values it advocates. Without them, OD represents nothing more than a set of techniques".

OD's Managerialist Perspective

OD, then, founded on participative philosophy and practices, aimed to free people from coercion. However, something happened along the way. Like other institutions such as law firms, health care and the church (Alvesson and Spicer, 2016), OD voluntarily surrendered its cultural autonomy and traditional values to managerialism. As David Boje (2012, p. 598) says,

> OD, change management, action research and all its cousins seems to have moved into the management camp, and don't know how to get out of all its colonizing, imperializing projects . . . In effect, they [OD practitioners] became too focused on what managers said.

Following Kurt Levin, continues Boje,

> OD created a generation of practitioners who saw their role as neutral change facilitators driven by a set of democratic and humanistic values . . . In the 1960s and 1970s this situation changed. Practitioners have become less neutral and more managerialist.

They became primarily concerned with implementing managers' vision and goals through working with members of the organization. In this reality, consultants have had difficulty maintaining OD's basic values, which traditionally considered the needs of all stakeholders in the organization. Warner Woodworth (1981) compares OD practitioners to CIA agents infiltrating organizations on behalf of managerial interests. Loren Baritz (1960) refers to industrial psychologists (close cousins of OD) as "servants of power". Maxim Voronov and Warner Woodworth (2012, p. 450) argue that the interests shared by OD and management is rooted in OD discourse which defines OD interventions as a top-down practice. In their words,

> We argue that a related contribution of the OD discourse to the cooptation of OD interventions by managerial interests is the insistence that OD interventions be managed from the top. This principle, in itself, privileges the managerial interests and legitimizes OD practitioners' doing the top executives' bidding with little regard to the impact of their intervention on the employees.
>
> (Voronov and Woodworth, 2012, p. 450)

Graeme Salaman (2002, p. 253) goes even further to claim that consultants contribute to managers' governability—they supply "theories and proposals for the constituents of governmentality" (see also Miller and Rose, 1994). Other writers argue that OD contributes to managers' governability in their marked use of therapeutic discourse and practices that focus on employees' self-development and growth in accordance with managers' expectations (Bradford and Porras, 2005; Farias and Johnson, 2000). A clear example is the frequent use of medical discourse that includes concepts such as anxiety, defense mechanisms and overcoming employees' resistance as means to medicalize and remedy organizations (Nord and Jermier, 1994; Schein, 1969, 1993). Although mainstream OD, including individually oriented scholars and practitioners, consider the group level (for instance, by using the concept of culture), I argue that the use of medical discourse relates mainly to an individual's psychological dispositions (anxiety or inner resistance). Specifically, I claim that the medical language very often assumes that the source of organizations' occurrences, events and problems is within the individual employees, who need to "work" on them*selves* and improve their personal skills and abilities. This assumption leaves managements' responsibility for the organizational problems out of sight (Coghlan, 2012; Voronov and Woodworth, 2012).

I find a precise example of the managerialist approach in the OD field in Edgar Schein's seminal book *Process Consultation* and more specifically in the book's subtitle: *Lessons for Managers and Consultants*. Dedicating the second edition of the book to managers, Schein says:

> In fact, one of the most powerful insights that managers obtained [by reading *Process Consultation*] was that they could influence situations without the direct use of power and formal authority . . . I believe that all managers can become more effective if they adopt some of the concepts of process consultation and learn some of the skills associated with that concepts.
>
> (Schein, 1987, p. viii)

I claim that by dedicating such a central book in the OD field to managers, Schein contributes openly to managers' ability to govern. Specifically, by directing his process-oriented ideas and practices such as active listening and overcoming resistance to managers only (and not to other participants in the organization), Schein, a significant OD scholar-practitioner who writes from the heart of the OD field, helps managers apply a symbolic violence that, as he says in the last extract, "could influence situations without the direct use of power and formal authority". By this, I argue, Schein indirectly (and I guess unintentionally) contributes to the reproduction of existing asymmetric power relations between managers and other employees and thus to non-democratic, non-ethical and non-productive change processes.

In a textual analysis of *Organizational Culture and Leadership*, Schein's (2010) other seminal book, Albert Mills and Tony Simmons (1995) see another example for the managerialist perspective. In this book, Mills and Simmons say, Schein makes a clear distinction between employees and managers. He defines employees largely by the term "*groups*" and managers by the term "*clients*" (of the consultation process). Using these definitions, OD consultants help employees (groups) adapt to external reality defined by the organization's doxa; those unquestioned assumptions that in practice are represented by the organization-specific habitus produced mainly by managers who are the clients of consultancy projects (Salaman, 2002, p. 253).

I should say that as an OD consultant, I have never felt that I enact a managerialist consulting approach. I haven't thought that I am participating in an imperialist colonial project, as Boje suggests, nor like a CIA agent infiltrating organizations to fulfill executive interests, as Woodworth (1981) describes OD consultants, and not as a "servant of power" as Baritz (1960) calls industrial psychologists. However, I believe that in the past, when I facilitated OD group workshops as part of change processes, I often voluntarily surrendered my consulting values to managers' needs, goals and interests. I offered my knowledge and perhaps more importantly my symbolic and cultural capitals that were given me for my expertise to the governance of those who bought my consulting services. Specifically, although through empathic listening and other therapeutic practices I have helped reduce (at least temporarily) non-manager employees' anxiety and anger, I also helped in overcoming their resistance to change, thus ignoring their perspectives. I realize now that I, the "objective" expert, the "impartial" consultant (as I believe I am), often exerted a symbolic violence that used "soft" therapeutic discourse and practice to impose management's understanding of the change process on non-manager employees who were my first clients, my immediate consultees (Fincham and Clark, 2002).

In short, following Bourdieu's theory of action, which focuses on uncovering hidden and taken-for-granted structures, I understand now that my consulting behavior in the past helped to enforce managers' knowledge and actions on non-managerial employees. Very often, I built employees' perspectives on the change process in terms defined by management's expectations, while disregarding questions of power relations that produced different perspectives between managers and employees on the very same change process that I was invited to help with.

OD as a Bridge Between Organizations and Society

I suspect, however, that although Bourdieu's theory of action helped me get rid of managerialist aspects of my consulting practice, some readers would argue that in general I misuse Bourdieu's theory. They would say that Bourdieu did not develop his theory and concepts to serve organizations (or OD projects) and to reproduce capitalist and neo-liberal injustice. Bourdieu's deep conclusions and logic are anti-capitalist and hostile to neo-liberal notions; hence, the use of his theory and concepts for the purpose of organization development disconnects them from their inner logic. It uses them for the opposite purpose of what Bourdieu intended.

The argument can continue this way: instead of using Bourdieu's critical concepts to point out where inequality is rooted, I use them to reproduce inequality by strengthening capitalism and neo-liberalism oiled machines. A reasonable use of Bourdieu's concepts, one that matches his spirit, would avoid the effort to achieve organization development and improvement. It would not serve as "a relay between societal discourses of the economy and programs and principles of organizational restructuring" (Salaman, 2002, p. 255), which is OD's raison d'être. Specifically, a reasonable use of Bourdieu's concepts should not "[s]upply a translation device between . . . change programs and wider socioeconomic discourses . . . [that] support internal processes of governmentality by aligning them with wider societal authoritative discourses of economic and political management" (Salaman, 2002, p. 255). Instead, use of Bourdieu's theory and concepts should focus on exposing the capitalist and neo-liberal assumptions and language on which organizations base their logic of action. As says Bourdieu, it ought to unmask the neo-liberal 'strong discourse'

> which is so strong and so hard to fight because it has behind it all the powers of a world of power relations which it helps to make as it is, in particular by orienting the economic choices of those who dominate economic relations and so adding its own—specifically symbolic—force to those power relations.
>
> (Bourdieu, 1998a, pp. 95–96)

I agree with this argument, but only partially. As an OD consultant, I work not only with "those who dominate economic relations". I also work with their employees, often contractual employees, to whom living under structural inequality of power is highly connected to personal fear (Knights and McCabe, 2002). If only for this reason, I believe I *should* use Bourdieu's theory and concepts in my consulting practice. Bourdieu helps me develop a consulting model, the HOOD that serves as a bridge between organizations and society. He helps me go back to OD's original democratic and humanistic values and practices and address "not only the individual, the group, and the organization but also the larger society" (Martin, 2016, p. 62). Specifically, Bourdieu helps me do both, expose the capitalist and neo-liberal injustice and develop discourse and practices to help individuals in organizations deeply understand and effectively cope with the often-invisible societal and structural mechanisms that produce this injustice.

Macro-Emancipation

However, I do not encourage OD scholars and practitioners to focus on changing the very existence of the capitalist and neo-liberal societal macro-economic structures. That is, I do not think OD should take a direct role in "macro-emancipation". Macro-emancipation, according to Mats Alvesson and Hugh Willmott (1992) entails "radical transformation of not only the workplace, but also society more generally". Specifically, I do not think OD's research and practice should or can directly confront "the policy of financial deregulation . . . the *structural violence* of unemployment, of insecure employment and of the *fear* provoked by the threat of losing employment" (Bourdieu, 1998a, pp. 96–98).

In my understanding, changing the discussed societal macro-economic structure is a big project, bigger than what I can do here and what OD in its current academic and practical form can do. Focusing on macro-emancipation is not only beyond OD's ability. It also has the potential to distract OD scholars and practitioners' attention away from restrictive structures that are on the level of the organization and in the here-and-now of the consulting process. Isabelle Huault, Veronique Perret, and André Spicer (2014, p. 41) write that "A strict focus on macro-emancipation tends to ignore many of the fleeting attempts to create limited zones of freedom which do not necessarily directly question broadly social structural modes of domination".

Micro-Emancipation

Reading Bourdieu's writings deeply provides hope. I find this hope in Bourdieu's claim that even in today's hyper capitalism there are social agents that actively work to promote a better social order, ones that do not focus only on achieving "selfish interests". In his words,

> And so if one can retain some reasonable hope, it is that, in state institutions and also in the dispositions of agents, there still exist forces which, under the appearance of simply defending a vanishing order and the corresponding 'privileges', will in fact, to withstand the pressure, have to work to invent and construct a social order which is not governed solely by the pursuit of selfish interest and individual profit, and which makes room for collectives oriented towards rational pursuit of collectively defined and approved ends.
> (Bourdieu, 1998a, p. 104)

I believe that OD can and should be one of the social agents to which Bourdieu is referring. From its place between organizations and society, OD, as a movement or a scholarly discipline, ought to use its cultural and symbolic capitals and humanistic and democratic values to limit the influence of the capitalist order on the level of the organization to help consultees work within the capitalist structure in relative freedom from its repressive structures. Specifically, OD can use its therapeutic and participative practices to create micro-emancipation that creates the local and temporal zones of freedom Huault, Perret, and Spicer (2014, p. 41) refer to, which "do not directly question broadly social structural modes of domination". Micro-emancipation happens, according to Alvesson and Willmott (2002),

> when employees have greater scope for arranging their own schedules and working practices, albeit with the parameters (e.g., quantity and quality targets) set by others. These changes invariably involve the removal of some oppressive restrictions even when or as they are accompanied by increased stress and job insecurity.
>
> (p. 624)

In order to create micro-emancipation OD should pay attention to "power relations, hierarchies, and privilege" (Voronov, 2005, p. 18) and uncover accepted assumptions and taken-for-granted social structures that shape consultees' thinking and behavior in the image of management and in accordance with efficiency and effectiveness. Emancipating consultees from the presumed structural level will help OD to apply change processes that do not suffer from the blaming and self-blaming effect. Specifically, these processes will create an ethical change that is not ruled only by self-centered interest and profit but serves the interests, the needs and the perspectives of many (Bourdieu, 1998a). As Burnes and Cooke (2012) write (see also Burnes and By, 2011),

> OD with its humanist, democratic and ethical values, wide range of participative tools and techniques, and experience in promoting behavior changes, is ideally placed not just to facilitate the 'Long Marches' such changes require, but also to play a leading role in the movement to a more ethical and sustainable future.

Allow me to expand further on the concept of micro-emancipation with another example from my own OD experience. As part of the current capitalist and neo-liberal demands, I founded eight years ago and now am heading an OD graduate program that some critics say serves capitalism and neo-liberalism. The program, they say, strategically trains future consultants to strengthen the capitalist and neo-liberal exploitative structures that cherish profit while ignoring the human side of change processes.

However, in line with the theoretical assumptions of this book, our curriculum includes both strategic *and* critical perspectives. The students read and use practically OD's action research methods and Edgar Schein's Process Consultation's intervention approach. At the same time, they reflect on these two specific strategic issues (action research and Process Consultation) by discussing Bourdieu's theory of practice and managerial and sociological critical literature.

Strictly saying, we are not only functional and strategic, showing our students nothing but how to change organizations. Instead, we try to develop their reflexivity to habitus and to social structure to enable them conduct effective and yet humane change processes. To this end, we encourage students to enact micro-emancipation processes that focus on the social and structural level of the organization. Emancipation, as we teach the students following Bourdieu (1998b) is a process of liberating individuals and groups from restrictive social structures that impose themselves on their thoughts and behaviors. Micro-emancipation in our classrooms thus means *releasing consultees' habitus as much as possible from the organization's structural constrains.*

More specifically, micro-emancipation in the way we teach OD means freeing consultees as much as possible from unequal power relations and distribution of resources that push non-management individuals and groups to the margins of the organization, preventing them from creatively contributing to the organization and from improving their position in the organization. In practice, this means using consulting meetings to question assumed structures of power and power relations and to challenge organizations' policy-makers, those powerful agents who drive capitalism and thus are able to deconstruct and reconstruct the capitalist system's conditions that in the name of profitability, effectiveness and economic profit, prevent non-management groups from freely acting and expressing their perspectives.

I believe that when I turned Omer's attention to the fact that his supportive and active listening enacted a symbolic violence that negated Benny's attempts to change the department's restrictive social structure and improve his position, I performed a pure micro-emancipation. That is, I liberated Omer's habitus from Kimono's doxa or unspoken reality in which workers should continually work on themselves and improve their personal skills and abilities in accordance with the organization's needs, as defined by the management. This specific emancipation process got practical meaning when Omer agreed to see Benny's resistance to fixing the department's faults not only as a psychological and private phenomenon reflecting Benny's psychological dispositions (low personal responsibility and commitment), but also as a sociological and collective phenomenon reflecting Benny's social dispositions, or habitus, that embodies Kimono's restrictive social structure.

Note

1 According to David Bradford and Warner Burke (2005b, p. 13), Richard Beckhard, Douglas MacGregor, Robert Blake and Herbert Shepard were the first to use the term Organization Development at the end of 1950s.

Bibliography

Alvesson, M. and A. W. Johansson (2002). Professionalism and politics in management consultancy work. In T. Clark and R. Fincham (Eds.), *Critical Consulting: New Perspectives on the Management Advice Industry.* (pp. 228–246). Oxford: Blackwell.

Alvesson, M. and A. Spicer (2016). Conditional surrender? Why do professionals willingly comply with managerialism? *Journal of Organizational Change Management,* 29(1), 29–45.

Alvesson, M. and H. Willmott (1992). On the idea of emancipation in management and organization studies. *Academy of Management Review,* 17(3), 432–464.

Alvesson, M. and H. Willmott (1996). *Making Sense of Management: A Critical Introduction.* Thousand Oaks, CA: Sage Publications.

Alvesson, M. and H. Willmott (2002). Identity regulation as organizational control: Producing the appropriate individual. *Journal of Management Studies,* 39(5), 619–644.

Anderson, D. L. (2015). *Organization Development: The Process of Leading Organizational Change.* Los Angeles, CA: Sage Publications.

Baldry, C. and A. Barnes (2012). The open-plan academy: Space, control and the undermining of professional identity. *Work, Employment and Society,* 26(2), 228–245.

Baritz, L. (1960). *The Servants of Power: A History of the Use of Social Science in American Industry.* Middletown, CT: Wesleyan University Press.

Bartunek, J. M. and M. K. Moch (1987). First-order, second-order, and third-order change and organization development interventions: A cognitive approach. *The Journal of Applied Behavioral Science,* 23(4), 483–500.

Bierema, L. L. (2010). *Implementing a Critical Approach to Organization Development.* Malabar, FL: Krieger.

Boje, D. M. (2012). Postscript. In D. M. Boje, B. Burnes and J. Hassard (Eds.), *The Routledge Companion to Organizational Change.* (pp. 45–58). London and New York: Routledge.

Boje, D. M. and G. A. Rosile (2001). Where's the power in empowerment? Answers from Follett and Clegg. *The Journal of Applied Behavioral Science,* 37(1), 90–117.

Bourdieu, P. (1998a). Neo-liberalism, the utopia (becoming a reality) of unlimited exploitation. In *Acts of Resistance: Against the Tyranny of the Market.* (pp. 95–105). New York: New Press.

Bourdieu, P. (1998b). On Television and Journalism. (Translated: Priscilla Parkhurst and Ferguson). London: Pluto.

Bradford, D. L. and W. W. Burke (2005a). The future of OD? In D. L. Bradford and W. W. Burke (Eds.), *Reinventing Organization Development: New Approaches to Change in Organizations.* (pp. 43–64). San Francisco, CA: Pfeiffer.

Bradford, D. L. and W. W. Burke (Eds.) (2005b). *Reinventing Organization Development: New Approaches to Change in Organizations.* New York: John Wiley & Sons.

Bradford, D. L. and J. I. Porras (2005). A historical view of the future of OD: An interview with Jerry I. Porras. In D. L. Bradford and W. W. Burke (Eds.), *Reinventing Organization Development: New Approaches to Change in Organizations.* (pp. 43–64). San Francisco, CA: Pfeiffer.

Burke, W. W. (1992). *Organization Development: A Process of Learning and Changing.* New York: Addison-Wesley.

Burke, W. W. (2008). *Organization Change: Theory and Practice.* Thousand Oaks, CA: Sage Publications.

Burke, W. W. (2010). A perspective on the field of organization development and change: The Zeigarnik effect. *The Journal of Applied Behavioral Science,* 47(2), 143–167.

Burnes, B. and D. Bargal (2017). Kurt Lewin: 70 years on. *Journal of Change Management,* 17(2), 91–100.

Burnes, B. and R. T. By (2011). Leadership and change: The case for greater ethical clarity. *Journal of Business Ethics,* 2, 239–253.

Burnes, B. and B. Cooke (2012). Review article: The past, present and future of organization development: Taking the long view. *Human Relation,* 65(11), 1395–1429.

Chauvière, M. and S. S. Mick (2013). The French sociological critique of managerialism: Themes and frameworks. *Critical Sociology,* 39(1), 135–143.

Chopra, R. (2003). Neoliberalism as doxa: Bourdieu's theory of the state and the contemporary Indian discourse on globalization and liberalization. *Cultural Studies,* 17(3–4), 419–444.

Church, A. H., J. Waclawski and W. Siegal (1996). Will the real OD practitioner please stand up? A call for change in the field. *Organization Development Journal,* 14(2), 5–14.

Clegg, S. (2014). Managerialism: Born in the USA. *Academy of Management Review,* 39(4), 566–576.

Coghlan, D. (2012). Organization development and action research: Then and now. In D. M. Boje, B. Burnes and J. Hassard (Eds.), *The Routledge Companion to Organizational Change.* (pp. 45–58). London and New York: Routledge.

Costea, B., N. Crump and K. Amiridis (2008). Managerialism, the therapeutic habitus and the self in contemporary organizing. *Human Relation,* 61(5), 661–685.

Cummings, T. G. (2005). Organization development and change: Foundations and applications. In J. Boonstra (Ed.), *Dynamics of Organizational Change and Learning.* New York: John Wiley.

Deetz, S. A. (1992). *Democracy in an Age of Corporate Colonization.* Albany, NY: State University of New York Press.

De Vos, J. (2010). Christopher Lasch's the culture of narcissism: The failure of a critique of psychological politics. *Theory & Psychology,* 20(4), 528–548.

Dobbin, F. (2008). The poverty of organizational theory: Comment on: Bourdieu and organizational analysis. *Theory and Society,* 37, 53–63.

Farias, G. and H. Johnson (2000). Setting the record straight. *The Journal of Applied Behavioral Science,* 36(3), 377–381.

Fincham, R. and T. Clark (2002). Introduction: The emergence of critical perspective on consulting. In T. Clark and R. Fincham (Eds.), *Critical Consulting: New Perspectives on the Management Advice Industry.* (pp. 1–18). Oxford: Blackwell.

Fleming, P. and A. Sturdy (2009). "Just be yourself!" Towards neo-normative control in organisations. *Employee Relations,* 31(6), 569–583.

French, Jr., J. R. P. and B. Raven (1977). The bases of social power. In H. L. Tosi and W. C. Hammer (Eds.), Organizational Behavior and Management: A Contingency Approach. (pp. 442–456). Chicago, IL: St. Clair Press.

Gergen, K. J., M. M. Gergen and J. F. Barrett (2004). Dialogue: Life and death of the organization. In D. Grant, C. Hardy, C. Oswick, N. Philips and L. Putnam (Eds.), *The Sage Handbook of Organizational Discourse.* (pp. 39–59). Thousand Oaks, CA: Sage Publications.

Gergen, K. J. and T. J. Thatchenkery (1996). Developing dialogue for discerning differences. *The Journal of Applied Behavioral Science*, 32(4), 428–433.

Glover, I. (2013). Bleak house: Pessimism and prescription about management, responsibility and society in the early 21st century. *Work, Employment & Society*, 27(2), 360–367.

Huault, I., V. Perret and A. Spicer (2014). Beyond macro-and micro-emancipation: Rethinking emancipation in organization studies. *Organization*, 21(1), 22–49.

Illouz, E. (2008). *Saving the Modern Soul: Therapy, Emotions, and the Culture of Self-help.* Berkeley, CA: University of California Press.

Klikauer, T. (2013). Managerialism and business schools-a review essay [Book Review]. *Australian Universities' Review*, 55(2), 128–132.

Klikauer, T. (2015). What is managerialism? *Critical Sociology*, 41(7–8), 1103–1119.

Knights, D. and D. McCabe (2002). A road less travelled: Beyond managerial, critical and processual approaches to total quality management. *Journal of Organizational Change*, 15(3), 235–254.

Locke, R. R. and J. C. Spender (2011). *Confronting Managerialism: How the Business Elite and Their Schools Threw Our Lives Out of Balance.* London and New York: Zed Books.

Lynch, K. (2014). New managerialism, neoliberalism and ranking. *Ethics in Science and Environmental Politics*, 13(2), 141–153.

Margulies, N. and A. Raia (1988). The significance of core values on the theory and practice of organizational development. *Journal of Organizational Change Management*, 1(1), 6–17.

Martin, M. (2016). Taking OD back to the future. *Organization Development Journal*, 34(2), 61.

Mick, S. (1973). Industrial Change and Industrial Conflict: The Case of the Plant That Would Not Die. Unpublished doctoral dissertation, Yale University, New Haven, CT.

Miller, P. and N. Rose (1994). On therapeutic authority: Psychoanalytical expertise under advanced liberalism. *History of the Human Sciences*, 7(3), 29–64.

Mills, A. J. and T. Simmons (1995). *Reading Organization Theory: A Critical Approach.* Toronto: Garamond.

Mills, A. J., T. Simmons and J. H. Mills (2010). *Reading Organization Theory: A Critical Approach to the Study of Organizational Behavior and Structure.* Ontario: The University of Toronto Press.

Mueller, F. and C. Carter (2007). 'We are all managers now': Managerialism and professional engineering in UK electricity utilities. *Accounting, Organizations and Society*, 32(1–2), 181–195.

Nord, W. R. and J. M. Jermier (1994). Overcoming resistance to resistance: Insights from a study of the shadows. *Public Administration Quarterly*, 17(4), 396–409.

Piotrowski, C. and T. R. Armstrong (2004). The research literature in organization development: Recent trends and current directions. *Organization Development Journal*, 22(2), 48.

Rose, N. (1991). *Experts of the Soul*, 91–99. Retrieved from http://journals.zpid. de/index.php/PuG/article/viewFile/103/142

Roy, W. G. (1999). *Socializing Capital: The Rise of the Large Industrial Corporation in America*. Princeton, NJ: Princeton University Press.

Salaman, G. (2002). Understanding advice: Toward a sociology of management consultancy. In T. Clark and R. Fincham (Eds.), *Critical Consulting: New Perspectives on the Management Advice Industry*. (pp. 247–259). Oxford: Blackwell.

Schein, E. H. (1969). *Process Consultation: Its Role in Organization Development*. Reading, MA: Addison-Wesley.

Schein, E. H. (1987). *Process Consulting: Lessons for Managers and Consultant*. (Vol. 1). Reading, MA: Addison-Wesley.

Schein, E. H. (1990). Back to the future: Recapturing the OD vision. In F. Massarik (Ed.), *Advances in Organization Development*. (Vol.1, pp. 13–26). Norwood, NJ: Ablex.

Schein, E. H. (1993). On dialogue, culture and organizational learning. *Reflections*, 4(4), 27–38.

Schein, E. H. (1999). *Process Consultation Revisited: Building the Helping Relationship*. Reading, MA: Addison-Wesley.

Schein, E. H. (2005). Organization development: A wedding of anthropology and Organization therapy. In D. L. Bradford and W. W. Burke (Eds.), *Reinventing Organization Development: New Approaches to Change in Organizations*. (pp. 131–144). San Francisco, CA: Pfeiffer.

Schein, E. H. (2010). *Organizational Culture and Leadership*. San Francisco, CA: Jossey-Bass.

Shimoni, B. (2017). A sociological perspective to organization development. *Organizational Dynamics*, 46, 165–170.

Shimoni, B. (forthcoming). 'Why the hell can't the system work efficiently and properly?' The transfer of business-oriented habitus to the philanthropic and education fields in Israel. *Journal of Nonprofit Education and Leadership*.

Sieweke, J. (2014). Pierre Bourdieu in management and organization studies: A citation context analysis and discussion of contributions. *Scandinavian Journal of Management,* 30(4), 532–543.

Voronov, M. (2005). Should critical management studies and organization development collaborate? Invitation to a contemplation. *Organization Management Journal*, 2(1), 4–26.

Voronov, M. (2008). Toward engaged critical management studies. *Organization*, 15(6), 939–945.

Voronov, M. and W. P. Woodworth (2012). OD discourse and domination. In D. M. Boje, B. Burnes and J. Hassard (Eds.), *The Routledge Companion to Organizational Change*. (pp. 440–455). London and New York: Routledge.

Willmott, H. (1987). Studying managerial work: A critique and a proposal. *Journal of Management Studies*, 24(3), 249–270.

Woodworth, W. (1981). Organizational consultants, conspirators, and colonizers. Group & Organization Studies, 6(1), 57–64.

5 HOOD and Resistance to Change (RTC)

The Chapter's Argument and Goal

In the previous two chapters,[1] I present Omer's perspective that sees Benny's resistance (to fix or report the department's problems before the visit of the external audit) as a result of psychological dispositions, low motivation and commitment. Framing Benny's resistance in individualistic and psychological terms led Omer to use therapeutic discourse and practices, mainly active listening, in order to overcome Benny's resistance and improve his behavior. Specifically, I claimed that Omer's active listening enacted symbolic violence, implicitly trying to regulate Benny's self and improve his behavior—his interpersonal communication, motivation and commitment. I argued that Omer's focus on fixing Benny's psychological dispositions ignored the social context. Omer himself, as well as Kimono's management, helped to produce and diffuse the stormy social structure that provided the habitus that generated Benny's resistant behavior.

Omer's individually oriented approach toward Benny's resistance, like the way individually oriented OD deals with resistance to change (RTC), encouraged me to go back to the literature and explore more deeply how OD understands the whole idea of RTC. I found that the three most prevalent perspectives in mainstream OD literature understands RTC in at least three ways. First, it is found within the individual's psychological dispositions such as anxiety, self-esteem, self-defense and identity (Schein, 1996; Zander, 1950). Second, it lies within the social context of organizational structure, job categories, compensation or the performance-appraisal system (Dent and Goldberg, 1999, p. 25; Kotter, 1995, p. 64). Third, it is created in the interactions between change creators and acceptors (Ford, Ford, and D'Amelio, 2008; Oreg, 2006).

The habitus-oriented perspective does not search for RTC within the individual, nor in the social context or between change agents' creators and acceptors. Instead, it sees resistance a product of habitus. Habitus, to remind the reader, is a cognitive construct representing not the personal or the social roots of thoughts and behavior (for instance, resistance to change) but the combined, dialectic roots of the two (Bourdieu, 1989). The goal of this chapter is then to present the HOOD's theoretical and practical approach, which defines RTC as a social practice (discourse or actions) produced and reproduced constantly by social agents' habitus.

Three Approaches to RTC

RTC and the Individual

Traditionally, OD scholars and practitioners have seen RTC as something within the individual, often believing that it reflects "attempts by individuals to protect themselves from change" (Zander, 1950; quoted by Burnes, 2015, p. 10). Dennis Scott and Cynthia Jaffe (1988; quoted by Bovey and Hede, 2001, p. 534) say individuals go through a reaction process when they are personally confronted with major organizational changes. This process, they continue, consists of four phases: "initial denial, resistance, gradual exploration, and eventual commitment". In the same spirit, Wayne Bovey and Andrew Hede (2001, p. 535) claim that "the failure of many large-scale corporate change programs can be traced directly to employees' resistance". Based on a wide review of the RTC literature, Eric Dent and Susan Goldberg (1999) say that RTC has always been treated as something inside the individual and represented in terms like fear, frustration, innate aggression, emotionality, mistrust, personality conflict and personal uncertainty.

Furthermore, the traditional approach considers resistance the enemy of change (Waddell and Sohal, 1998, p. 546). It sees resistance, as Celine Bareil (2013, p. 61) says, as an obstacle, a problem to be removed, an anti-change behavior, or a threat on the part of a change recipient, usually an employee, who has a natural disposition to resist change. Specifically, resistance is seen as pathological, something that change creators need to overcome. The need to overcome resistance, Walter Nord and John Jermier (1994, p. 399) tell us, most probably comes from the Freudian use of "resistance", which sees resistance as the process that helps neurotic individuals to stay remote from reality and from taking the suggestions of their therapists. This process portrays resistance as irrational and as against change, which is without doubt a good thing. Once resistance is constructed in psychological terms, solutions are also psychological and in the form of therapeutic practices (Voronov and Woodworth, 2012). A concrete example of seeing resistance in psychological terms is Edgar Schein's (1987) OD model Process Consultation. According to Schein, the main role of consultants is to help managers (consultees) overcome the defense and denial evoked by processes of organizational change (Fincham and Clark, 2002). Specifically, Schein (1987), encourages consultants to develop clinical skills (e.g., empathetic listening, self-awareness and personal communication) in order to overcome what he calls the "resentment and defensiveness" of consultees toward the change process. Schein also encourages consultants to treat consultees in a sensitive way and build relationships with them based on trust and a safe psychological environment in order to overcome their resistance and continue with the change process.

The traditional approach, then, portrays resistance as mainly emotional, as we see in Chris Argyris and Donald Schon's (1974) assertion that resistance arises from defensive routines, from thoughts and behaviors aiming to protect individuals', groups' and organizations' routine patterns of coping with the social reality. Sandy Kristin Piderit (2000, pp. 785–786) argues that the concepts of frustration and anxiety are the infrastructure of Argyris and Schon's (1974) defensive routines. The two researchers, says Piderit, are preoccupied with the role of the external consultant in exposing and minimizing the anxiety that strengthens participants' defensiveness, which is inherent in those routines.

Limitations of the Traditional Approach

The understanding of individuals' psychological state in processes of change is, of course, important. These processes, in which individuals move from the known to the unknown, often produce frustration and anxiety manifested in explicit aggression and resistance. Change agents, managers and consultants need to be aware of these reactions and use practices such as participation and sharing of information about the change process that potentially can create a "safe psychological" environment (Schein, 2000, p. 37), a "climate" in which the consultees are able to produce effective change (Coghlan, 1993, p. 12).

However, as the literature shows and as I have found in my own consulting experience, viewing an individual's psychological dispositions as a starting point in understanding and coping with RTC is problematic since often it

- produces a resistance of itself.
- fails to see resistors as a source of knowledge and alternative agendas.
- ignores the part of the social context that is creating RTC.

Producing Resistance of Itself

As several scholars of resistance assert, viewing resistance as something within the individual and using therapeutic practices to overcome resistance by changing or curing individuals often generate the very resist-ance managers or other change agents are trying to overcome (Bareil, 2013; Ford, Ford, and D'Amelio, 2008; Jansen, 2000, p. 53). In other words, approaching individuals who are the main producers of RTC as resistors implicitly defines them as subjects who need remediation— they themselves are the problem that needs fixing. These definitions, as advocates of Appreciative Inquiry claim, (Boyd and Bright, 2007), can make consultees suspicious of the change process and of consultants and therefore escalate their fear and anxiety and generate resistance of itself. I believe that this is one reason that during the 1970s, managers resisted participating in T-Groups workshops which became (after the death of OD's founding father, Kurt Lewin) sites for transforming people and making them "psychologically healthier" as says David Porras (Bradford and Porras, 2005, p. 46). It is a "therapy" given to managers who are not interested in personal but in organizational treatment (Schein, 2005).

Resistance as a Resource

By regarding resistance as essentially bad, change agents, according to Jeffery Ford, Laurie Ford and Angelo D'Amelio (2008, p. 363), "have missed the potential contribution of increasing the likelihood of success-ful implementation, helping build awareness and momentum for change and eliminating unnecessary, impractical, or counterproductive elements in the design or conduct of the change process". Furthermore, Dianne Waddell and Amrik Sohal (1998, p. 545) say that resistance plays a crucial role in drawing attention to aspects of change that may be inappropriate, not well thought through, or perhaps plain wrong. By bypassing resist-ance, Nord and Jermier (1994, p. 399) argue, scholars and practitioners fail to see alternative perspectives, what they define as "viable alternative agendas". Scholars and practitioners therefore should perceive resistance as feedback and as a source of energy for organizations and as a "viable" part of the development of organizations (Ford and Ford, 2009).

Ignorance of the Social Context

The focus on individuals' psychological dispositions in understanding and coping with RTC often shows individuals to be the main source of practice and meaning. This perspective largely serves as an organiz-ing principle in individually oriented OD (Bradford and Porras, 2005). It assumes that if individuals do the best they can (by developing their working abilities and skills) they will always get positive results (Illouz, 2007). This assumption, which apparently reflects western individualistic notions of self and personal responsibility, tends very often to "blame" the individual for her or his behaviors, including those behaviors that were forced on them in specific social contexts (Gergen, Gergen, and

Barrett, 2004). In other words, according to this assumption, if individuals are the main source of meaning, they are also responsible for any kind of resistance, including resistance that the social context generates (by structures such as systems of rewards, allocation of resources and performance evaluation, Kotter, 1990).

I should say that today, after a long consulting career, research and teaching in which I have used Pierre Bourdieu's sociological terminology, I have learned that in my intensive use of therapeutic psychological discourse and practices I often assumed that participants' behavior generally reflect internal resistance that I should help organizations to overcome. Often, this discourse ("what do you feel about the change process?") and practice (group workshops in which participants share their feelings about the change process) helped participants go through the change process. However, most often the therapeutic discourse and practices blamed participants for their inner resistance while ignoring the part of the social context that produced that resistance. For example, when consultees complained that social context properties such as unequal systems of rewards, marginalization of the organization's structures or a strong and paralyzing management prevented them from achieving sufficient performance results (or fulfilling their own interests), my tendency was to 'invite' them to think of the external attribution they were doing. That is, pay attention to the projection process in which they put the responsibility for insufficient performance on the social context while not taking personal responsibility.

I understand now that my interpretation, in which I differentiated between responsible and not responsible people while ignoring the social context, along with the guilt I provoked among my consultees for their decision to 'escape' responsibility, helped me overcome their resistance and achieve agreement to improve their behavior and take responsibility for the poor results. The participants' agreement to change their behavior then helped me to perform processes of organizational change that were generated by those who invited me, mainly the managers of the organization, those who have the greatest control of the social structure, while marginalizing (and often excluding) the participants' perspectives which see those specific structures to be the reason for their resistance. In short, the focus on self-development as a way to overcome resistance often distracted my consultees' attention, as well as mine, from the social context's role in fostering RTC.

RTC and Social Context

S. M. Herman (1990, quoted by Coghlan, 1993, p. 10) criticizes what he calls "system viewpoint". He argues that "there is a distinct possibility that the organizational development and training functions have been seduced by the 'system viewpoint', and have lost sight of the importance of developing and training autonomous individuals". Herman's complaints about the dominance of the system perspective represent the parallel use by OD scholars and practitioners of the individual and the systemic orientations.

Going back to OD's roots, to Kurt Lewin's concept of field, Dent and Goldberg (1999, p. 25) claim that more and more researchers have begun seeing resistance as a "systems concept" in which resistance comes not from the individual, but from the context in which the change occurs (Burnes, 2015, p. 100). According to the two researchers, this happened when psychological concepts that focus mainly on an individual's dispositions replaced the former systems concepts. Kurt Lewin, according to Dent and Goldberg, did not search for individuals' motivations and resistance but for the social conditions and forces that work for or against change. For Lewin, they remind us, life in organizations, as in any other social group, is primarily a system of roles, positions, behaviors, social norms and other structural elements. In this life, in Lewin's words, "individual and group behavior is the product of a complex system or field of forces that surround individuals and form a force field or life space" (Quoted by Burnes, 2015, p. 100).

According to Burnes (2015), OD scholars and practitioners then began to consider the role of structure and culture in processes of organizational change and resistance (Peters and Waterman, 1982; Schein, 2010). Michael Beer, Russel Eisenstat, and Bert Spector (1990, p. 5), supporters of the structure approach, advocate putting workers into new organizational contexts that "impose" on them new ideas, responsibilities and relationships rather than focusing on individual behavior. Peter Senge (1990) claims that resistance to change occurs when the changers have not identified a balancing process so the change can be effective. Based on wide empirical research, John Kotter (1990) shows that workers often understand the direction of changes generated by firms' leaders and they are interested in helping to achieve those changes. At the same time, there are obstacles that prevent change from taking place. Such obstacles can be within individuals, but this is rare. More often, the obstacles lie in the organization's structure, which forces people to choose new perspectives at the expense of their own interests (Burnes, 2015; Dent and Goldberg, 1999). For example, narrow job categories can seriously undermine efforts to increase productivity or make it very difficult to consider customers, while performance-appraisal systems make people choose between the new vision and their own self-interest (Kotter, 1995, p. 64).

Supporters of the culture approach see inappropriate cultures and structures as either obstacles or opportunities for change processes and advise organizations to dismiss or replace employees who do not fit the desired cultures or structures (Burnes, 2015; French and Bell, 1999; Peters and Waterman, 1982). This is one way to understand the concept of organizational culture as defined by Edgar Schein, one of the prominent leaders in the OD field. Schein (2010, p. 3) sees an organization's culture as a pattern of common assumptions that have the potential to reduce resistance by showing the organization's members how to perceive, feel and act so as to "maintain the social order". In the same vein, examining the relationships among creativity, resistance to change, and social context in Chinese organizations, Alice Hon, Matt Bloom, and Michael Crant (2014, p. 934) conclude that organizational climate "might help overcome the effects of resistance to change".

RTC and Social Construction

The two approaches discussed here (the traditional and the social context), which separately serve OD scholars and practitioners as legitimate theoretical and practical perspectives to use to explain processes of RTC, view the personal and the social as relatively separated. Indeed, most empirical studies of resistance have barely focused on the mutual role of context and individuals in predicting employees' behavior in a time of organizational changes (Coghlan, 1993; Oreg, 2006). For the social construction approach, this separation, which views resistance as an either-or situation, within the individual or in the social context, is problematic since it misses the opportunity to see the relationship between the two in generating RTC. Bernard Burnes (2015, p. 103) says, "the individual and the systemic views of resistance need not be seen as irreconcilable per se". "Organizations", Burnes continues, "are social systems and therefore we should see resistance as emerging from the interplay between the characteristics of the individual and the characteristics of the organization" (see also Dent and Goldberg, 1999; Ford and Ford, 2010).

The social construction approach, then, sees the origins of RTC in the interaction between the personality and other personal motivations and the social context (Coghlan, 1993). John Kotter and Leonard Schlesinger (2008), for example, see "parochial self-interest, misunderstanding and lack of trust, different assessment of what change is needed and a low tolerance for change as important sources of resistance". An examination of their list, according to David Coghlan (1993, p. 11) shows that resistance lies in the personality as well as in the environment.

From a psychological perspective, Chris Argyris (1990; Coghlan, 1993, p. 11) connects the individual and the social context by viewing RTC as a psychological structure of organizations. For him, psychological structures of organizations, such as a low degree of openness, trust and risk taking, and a high degree of conformity and mistrust, construct concealed defensive routines and build systems to keep those defensive routines in place. When they show how dispositional resistance (the natural tendency of people to resist change) is always moderated by contextual factors such as the role of the change agents and the way in which they manage the change process, Alexandra Michel, Rune Todnem By, and Bernard Burnes (2013) also connect individuals' resistance and the social context (Burnes, 2015; Oreg, 2003). For them as well, as I understand it, RTC is a social construction that takes place in interactions between change creators and change acceptors. In referring to Kurt Lewin, Shaul Oreg (2006) claims that in any human interaction, possible sources of resistance are both within the individual and in the individual's environment. For him, when those in a worker's social environment (i.e., colleagues, supervisors and subordinates) tend to resist change, the worker will probably resist as well. However, Oreg (2003) maintains that although all individuals are disposed to resist change, some are more disposed to resist than others (Burnes, 2015). Individuals who are predisposed to RTC develop negative attitudes toward change processes and most often do not willingly participate in these processes (Oreg, 2003). At the same time, understanding an individual's level of dispositional resistance is not enough to imagine his/her resistance to change. An individual's dispositional resistance is always moderated by change agents' management style and by the change acceptors' involvement in the change process (see also Buchanan and Boddy, 1992; Hon, Bloom, and Crant, 2014).

From a sociological perspective, Waddell and Sohal (1998, p. 544) conclude that rather than being simply driven by self-interest, employees' resistance is constructed of a variety of social and management factors. In the same spirit, Ford, Ford, and D'Amelio (2008, p. 362) claim that the traditional approach to resistance, what they call the "change agent-centric view", assumes that resistance is a "reliable representation" by change agents (managers or consultants) of a neutral reality. They say that this assumption represents a tendency among scholars and practitioners to adopt the change agents' perspective, assuming that they are doing the right thing even as the change acceptors are putting up obstacles. In other words, the change agent-centric view does not see the change agents as actors who construct their social realities. For example, when workers experience loss of trust, injustice, broken agreements or betrayal they react in several ineffective ways, among them resentment, thievery, lower productivity and resistance. Change agents, Ford, Ford, and D'Amelio (2008, p. 362) conclude, "contribute to the occurrence of what they call resistant behavior . . . through their own actions and inactions, owing to their own ignorance, incompetence, or mismanagement". Resistance to the social construction approach, then, is actually a transaction between change producers and receivers.

Limitations of the Social Construction Approach

Researchers of resistance as a social construction explicitly or implicitly celebrate Kurt Lewin's return to the forefront of the field. They tell us that like Lewin they are conscious of the role of the social context and its interaction with the individual in generating processes of RTC. Oreg (2006) says resistance lies within the individual as well as in the individual's environment; Burnes (2015) says that contextual factors moderate dispositional resistance, and Ford, Ford, and D'Amelio (2008, p. 362) say that resistance occurs "between" change agents and change recipients. However, while returning to Lewin's ideas, researchers of the social construction approach fail to recognize two problems. First, they adopt his dichotomist and static view that perceives the social context and the individual in dichotomist terms, as two separated entities. Second, in their heavy reliance on subjectivity, they leave out Lewin's materiality approach (Boje, DuRant, Coppedge, Chambers, and Marcillo, 2011, p. 584).

The Dichotomist View

It seems that although the social construction approach recognizes the interplay between individuals and organizations' contexts, it views them as separate entities, externally defined and internally cohesive, that can only temporarily change. That is, during the change (or the resistance) process managers locally create (Ford, Ford, and D'Amelio, 2008) or temporarily moderate (Oreg, 2003; Oreg, Vakola, and Armenakis, 2011) workers' resistance. Specifically, borrowing Dent and Goldberg's (1999, p. 25) criticism of the traditional perspective on RTC, I would say that the social construction approach continues to see resistance as a situation of the employees versus managers. Moreover, I claim that beside this manager-centered view, which regularly sees managers or other change agents as responsible for setting the conditions necessary for the change process, to define workers' resistance as generated or moderated by change agents is to draw a one-dimensional picture of RTC. In this picture, resistance is always on the workers' side waiting to be produced or weakened by managers. Apparently, other participants in the organization also resist change. For example, people in positions of power may use organizational resources to resist changing the status quo (Dent and Goldberg, 1999). I assume, as well, that the picture social construction researchers draw is barely able to represent the resistance of middle managers who blame executives above them for resisting change (Spreitzer and Quinn, 1996).

Similarly, we cannot simply assume that workers are the only resistors in disputes over wages and other welfare conditions between managements and labor associations (Voronov and Woodworth, 2012). That is, representing the social context in terms of change agents, or managers, views resistance as an interpersonal construct, static and local, one that belongs to a specific change process. Such a view, I claim, is indifferent to the dynamic and changing nature of resistance. Resistance, as I show in detail in the

Table 5.1 Four approaches to resistance to change

Name of approach	Location of resistance	Description
The traditional approach	Within the individual	"What causes us to react defensively is a second kind of anxiety . . . learning anxiety, or the feeling that if we allow ourselves to enter a learning or a change process . . . we will lose our effectiveness, our self-esteem, and maybe our identity". Edgar Schein (1996, p. 60)
The social context approach	In the social context	"Sometimes the obstacle is the organizational structure: narrow job categories can seriously undermine efforts to increase productivity . . . Sometimes compensation or performance-appraisal system makes people choose between the new vision and their own self-interest". John Kotter (1995, p. 64)
The social construction approach	*The psychological orientation:* Within the individual's psychological dispositions moderated by managers	"As in regard to any human reaction, potential sources of resistance lie both within the individual as well as in the individual's environment". Shaul Oreg (2006, p. 74)
	The sociological orientation: In the interaction between change agents and change recipients	"Change agents contribute to the occurrence of what they call resistant behavior . . . through their own actions and inactions, owing to their own ignorance, incompetence, or mismanagement". Ford, Jeffrey, D., Laurie W. Ford, and Angelo D'Amelio (2008, p. 362)
The HOOD approach	Within the individual's habitus (social dispositions)	Resistance is a social practice built into the system, produced by social agents' habitus, historically developed in constant interactions between human agents and social structures in a given social field

See Shimoni, 2017

next section, is not a local reaction to specific change efforts but a routine social practice produced by social agents' habitus, historically developed in dialectical relations between social agents and social structures.

Neglecting Materiality

As already mentioned, the social construction approach to RTC often defines the organization's social context in human terms—managers

(Oreg, Vakola, and Armenakis, 2011), change agents (Ford and Ford, 2010) and changers (Senge, 1990). By reducing the social context to human agents, I argue that these writers do not fully adopt Lewin's sense of the social context. That is, they adopt Lewin's systemic and contextual view but leave out his concern for materiality. For Lewin, managers and other influential change agents do serve as a significant part of the social context in fostering or restraining RTC. However, human change agents are not the only actors in the performance of resistance. Social context, including material factors such as structures of tasks, formalization procedures, technical and bureaucratic control of work (allocation of resources, systems of rewards), take significant part in driving or restraining change (Alvesson, 2012).

To be more concrete, social constructionists often do recognize material factors such as allocation of resources and systems of rewards. However, their direct methodology and interest reflect an interpretative (sensemaking) and individual-centric view that focuses on attitudes (Piderit, 2000), behavior (Ford and Ford, 2010) and psychological dispositions (Oreg, Vakola, and Armenakis, 2011) that do not consider materiality. Following criticism of Kenneth Gergen and Karl Weick's use of social construction in change management research (Boje, DuRant, Coppedge, Chambers, and Marcillo (2011, p. 580), I would say that the subjective perception that social constructionists use depicts resistance mainly as a result of personal interactions between change agents and change acceptors. This construction, as I show in detail in the next section, ignores the role played by the organization's material conditions (control over resources, jobs definition and position in the organization) in producing RTC.

Case Study: Kimono

In 2008, David, a member of "Kimono's" board of directors, invited me to improve the firm's poor performance. Kimono is an Israeli firm owned by two business groups, Adventure, and Genesis that develops marine products for export to Western Europe and Japan. David and others in Kimono identified two people who they believed were responsible for the company's poor performance: John and Bill. John, one of Genesis' owners (with Wolf and Nathan), was the head of the marketing department and Bill, from Adventure, was the CEO. Adam described John and Bill's "problematic personalities", ineffective communication and strong resistance to changing their behavior:

> In a board meeting: if John and Bill will not sit together, we will not get anywhere.

Adam owns Genesis, and Brian and David were senior managers at Genesis. John, David, Nathan, Adam, Brian and Wolf served as Kimono's board members. My consulting role was to help John and Bill develop better interpersonal communication in order to improve Kimono's poor performance, or as I understood it, to help Kimono overcome John and Bill's resistance to changing their behavior:

> David [in a board meeting]: I am very angry. We come to a meeting and you both [John and Bill] are not coordinated . . . [Looking at me, saying:] This situation must change . . . You are raising a problem that is the reason for inviting the consultant [me].

As is common among OD practitioners, I conducted interviews with John and Bill and with all Kimono's board members, and participated in board meetings. The interviews indicated that John and Bill's interpersonal communication was indeed ineffective, something they strongly resisted changing:

BILL: Now I am fighting to get rid of John . . . I have no intention to waste my time sitting with him.
JOHN: Bill should stop behaving like a bodyguard . . . the Japanese decide what clean seaweed is, not Bill.

However, from the interviews I also learned about Kimono's stormy social and political context; that is, about the constant power struggles between Adventure and Genesis, the two business groups that own Kimono. These struggles, I found, started years ago with fights over issues such as Kimono's decision-making process, its strategic directions and operational processes:

JOHN: why are we here? Anyway, Adam will decide.
ADAM: I live in peace with saying such as "everything we do, Adam will decide differently" . . . there is a need to create a synergy between my head and their head.
BRIAN: we decided that Japan is our bread and butter and not the rest of the world.
DAVID: I do not remember that we decided to leave the world and focus only on Japan.

My research also showed that the board members, fully comprised of Adventure and Genesis' owners and deeply involved in Kimono's everyday management, were using John (Adventure) and Bill (Genesis) as a way to achieve each owner group's specific interests:

JOHN: Bill's best tool is his friendship with Adam . . . not everything he does is pure business.

BRIAN: I am very disappointed . . . he [John] visits abroad and we (Genesis) do not know anything about it.

At this point, my impression was that the source of John and Bill's ineffective communication and of their resistance to changing this communication (and therefore for Kimono's poor performance) was not only in their internal psychological dispositions, but also and perhaps mainly within the board. That is, the problem lay within the struggles between the two owner groups in which John and Bill fought for each owner group's specific interests.

RTC and HOOD

As we see in the case study, John and Bill's resistance to stopping their ineffective communication was not necessarily a result of psychological dispositions—of their "problematic personalities" as David said in the beginning. Rather, John and Bill's resistance was generated primarily by their habitus, the social dispositions they adopted from Kimono's social structures, such as a competitive worldview and a zero-sum-game perspective.

Furthermore, I claim that John and Bill's habitus was produced through constant struggles among participants in the two owner groups, Adventure and Genesis. I found that each of the interest groups (Adventure and Genesis) strongly attempted to fulfill its specific needs and interests through uncompromising struggles for control over types of capital and material resources and for improving its position. Specifically, I claim that the struggles between the two groups produced and diffused a social structure that through the participants' habitus intensely encouraged competition and struggle. This habitus (social dispositions) largely predisposed their fighting and uncooperative behavior. As Bourdieu (1993, p. 82) reminds us, social interactions never take place in a social vacuum. What happens between two persons is always well ordered by the objective relations between the two groups (for instance, class or gender) to which these two persons belong (Bourdieu and Wacquant, 1992, p. 97).

I argue, then, that understanding John and Bill's resistance to changing their ineffective communication requires first that we understand Kimono's social structure and the power struggles in which John and Bill's habitus has been formed. Indeed, the more I learned about the struggles in Kimono, the more I refused to see John and Bill's resistance to changing their nonfunctional behavior as a psychological construct in which two people, detached from the social structure, simply did not find the needed personal skills to approach each other effectively. Instead, John and Bill's resistance was dynamically formed with and against Kimono's turbulent social structure as expressed by the constant struggles over capitals, resources and positions. From the HOOD's perspective, then, resistance is not simply a reaction to specific change efforts but a social practice built into the system, produced by social agents' habitus historically developed in accordance with power relations and struggles in a given social field.

Another aspect of the social structure's role in producing John and Bill's resistance to changing their ineffective communication is John and Bill's problematic jobs definition as dictated by the board. Bill, an employee, was the CEO and as such in a higher operational position than John, one of Adventure's owners who was head of the marketing department. As CEO, Bill tried to manage Kimono as a whole, including the marketing department headed by John. John refused to accept Bill's leadership, claiming that he was not willing to take instructions from an employee.

Advocates of the social context approach to RTC would correctly claim that John and Bill's problematic job definitions (in which Bill, an employee, is in charge of John, an owner) is largely responsible for the ineffective communication and for their resistance to changing this communication. Using the habitus concept, however, allowed me to go deeper into the problem. I would suggest that as a CEO, Bill held habitus dispositions that generated a strong will to manage Kimono as a whole, including John. John, in opposition, held owner habitus dispositions that generated expectations of getting routine reports from any employee in the organization, including Bill. I claim that John and Bill's different habitus generated conflictual thoughts and expectations that in turn produced their resistance to changing their aggressive and ineffective communication. John and Bill, then, worked in deep structural constraints. The internalization of these constraints into their habitus, their social dispositions, I argue, left them almost no option but to rely on their symbolic and material resources and on their positions and roles (one an owner and the other a CEO) and enact ineffective communication and resistance to changing that communication.

In my interviews and active participation in the board meetings, though, I found that John and Bill's resisting behavior was not only a direct reaction to Kimono's social structures. The two were not powerless agents that simply applied Kimono's social structure against their will. Instead, by ignoring each other, hiding information and eroding each other's professional legitimacy they creatively refined and 'improved' their (contested) habitus that in its turn reproduced Kimono's combative social structure. Social agents, as Bourdieu (1989) tells us, do not respond mechanically to the social structure. Instead, they used creative strategies to gain control over capitals and positions and to *re*produce their own combative habitus and the social structure in which this habitus develops.

The focus on habitus thus enabled me to take the responsibility for Kimono's poor performance off John and Bill's shoulders, off their resistance, and yet not to leave the responsibility only on the owners' shoulders. It enabled me to go to Kimono's cognitive world in which the dichotomy of social versus personal does not exist; that is, to the place in which constant struggles for capital and competition over resources (among all participants, including John and Bill) were incorporated into John and Bill's resisting thought and behavior. For Bourdieu (1996, p. 38) "the most obscure principle of action . . . lies neither in structures nor in consciousness, but rather in the relation of immediate proximity between objective structures and embodied structures—in habitus" (See also Lizardo, 2004, p. 381).

In this chapter then I understand resistance to be an integral part of both the individual and the organization. This integration transcends dichotomist constructions, "dualities", in Bourdieu's language, and sees resistance as a mix of the internal, subjective, personal and private with the external, objective, social and public. More specifically, like any OD intervention practice, HOOD is interested in the resistors' subjectivity. However, habitus expands this subjectivity to include not only psychological but also social dispositions that are not only internal and private but also external and public, representing not the personal *or* the social roots of resistance but the *combined, dialectic*, roots of the two (Lahire, 2002).

By considering participants' subjectivity as not only internal and private but also external and public, HOOD encourages OD practitioners not to try to overcome or suppress what the traditional approach defines as an inner (personal) RTC. Instead, it encourages them to use RTC as a source of information about the structural conditions that take part in producing and establishing resistance in organizations. At Kimono, I did not perceive John and Bill's resistance as private and personal, and hence did not try to overcome or suppress this resistance. Instead, I used their resistance as a source of information about the joint responsibility of their own behavior and the structural conditions in which they live, mainly the struggles between the owner groups and their conflicting job definitions.

I can only guess that if I had followed the traditional approach to RTC and focused on "fixing" John and Bill and their ineffective communication, as David expected, I would, perhaps, have helped Kimono overcome John and Bill's resistance to working together. However, I also might have faced the same problems the traditional approach suffers from. First, *by* 'blaming' only *John and Bill* for their aggressive and ineffective communication and by *regarding* this kind of communication as *something bad* (e.g., as *the* reason for Kimono's poor performance) *that needed fixing* I would have taken the risk of producing a new resistance. Second, by trying to fix John and Bill and overcoming or bypassing their resistance, I would have *missed the opportunity to learn about* the different agendas each owner group had and the roles of John and Bill in fulfilling these agendas. Third, by focusing only on John and Bill's communication I would not have identified the part played by Kimono's structural conditions (mainly, the struggles among the owner groups and John and Bill's conflicting job definitions) in producing their resisting behavior.

In practice, understanding John and Bill's RTC as a product of Kimono's structural conditions and contested habitus encouraged me to define Kimono's board (and not John and Bill) as the "primary client" (Schein, 1991, p. 65) who should have responsibility for Kimono's poor performance and for the development of structural changes. As a means of developing and implementing those changes, I used the weekly board meetings to develop a new and agreed-upon business plan, new rules and regulations for effective board meetings, a clear agenda for each meeting and a follow-up decision-making process.

Using the concept of habitus, then, allows OD practitioners to search for resistance not only among workers but also among other participants, such as Kimono's owner groups. In contrast to concepts such as self and personality, habitus does not recognize boundaries such as the individual's body or role, and even not of department, organization or field in which the organization is socially located. Every habitus (including managers' and owners') is embodied in a wider social context and is therefore influenced by the social structures of that context. At Kimono, the habitus orientation enabled me to learn about the social structure's part in producing not only John and Bill's habitus and resistance but also the board members' habitus and resistance (to compromise in their daily mutual interactions) that played a significant role in generating John and Bill's resistance.

What are the theoretical contributions of HOOD to understanding RTC? The three most prevalent perspectives see RTC as a product of psychological dispositions (*the traditional*), structural factors (*the social context*) and interactions between creators and acceptors of change (*the social construction*). For the HOOD, on the contrary, resistance is a frequent social practice that has been developed and institutionalized in the organization's social field and in the habitus of its social agents. That is, resistance is always out there in the field. It should not be seen as a surprise but as an existing and dynamic phenomenon that does not wait for the change agents to come or for the change process to begin. The beginning of the change process only exposes structured resistance and makes it public.

Resistance is also not a local reaction to specific change efforts but a social practice built into the system, produced by social agents' habitus that has been historically developed in dialectical relations between agents and structures in a given social field. Through these interactions, social agents use their symbolic and material capitals and constantly develop and enact resistance strategies to maintain or to change the field's (organization) power relations while protecting and/or improving their position in the organization's social structure. Understanding resistance from the HOOD perspective thus entails an investigation of the organization's social field and its symbolic and material structures in restraining and fostering change.

What are the practical implications? It seems that a focus on participants' social and not on psychological dispositions (habitus) provides OD with a valuable tool for understanding and coping with RTC in at least three practical directions. First, a focus on social dispositions enables us to apply what I define as a *fair change process.* In a fair change process, social agents are not the only factor responsible for the organization's faults and do not need to improve constantly as a means to curing these faults while the organization itself remains untreated (Illouz, 2007). Applying the fair change process in the case of John and Bill helped me to define their resistance as not only a personal but also an organizational problem, a problem that represents the role of Kimono's strong structural forces in producing John and Bill's habitus and resistance to changing their behavior.

Second, a focus on resistors' social dispositions has a good potential to release us from the individualistic perception of self and personal responsibility that largely dominates the OD field. That perception sees the individual as the main source of meanings and actions including those meanings and actions that were forced on her or him in specific social contexts (Gergen, Gergen, and Barrett, 2004). To be more specific, the focus on social dispositions can slow the accepted tendency among OD practitioners and managers to view resistors as *patients* with personal pathologies (e.g., John and Bill's *"problematic personalities"* as David called them) who need cure and remedy. At the same time, putting the social dispositions at the center encourages researchers, practitioners and managers to consider the social context as a significant source of meanings and actions and the resistors' viewpoints and alternative agendas as useful knowledge for the development of the organization.

Third, a focus on resistors' social dispositions can prevent the production of new resistance. I believe that John and Bill did not resist working with me since I focused on their social and not psychological dispositions. That is, my motivation to search not only for the internal roots of their resistance but for the external ones as well was accepted by them as honest consulting practice aimed at learning in depth what their resistance really demonstrated, and not attributing Kimono's poor performance only to them.

Notes

1 The chapter is based on Shimoni (2017).

Bibliography

Alvesson, M. (2012). *Understanding Organizational Culture*. Los Angeles, CA: Sage Publications.

Argyris, C. (1990). *Overcoming Organizational Defenses*. Boston, MA: Allyn and Bacon.

Argyris, C. and D. A. Schon (1974). *Theory in Practice: Increasing Professional Effectiveness*. San Francisco, CA: Jossey-Bass.

Bareil, C. (2013). Two paradigms about resistance to change. *Organization Development Journal*, 31(3), 59–71.

Beer, M., R. A. Eisenstat and B. Spector (1990). Why change programs don't produce change. *Harvard Business Review*, 68(6), 4–12.

Boje, D., M. L. DuRant, K. Coppedge, T. Chambers and M. Marcillo-Gomez (2011). Social materiality: A new direction in change management and action research. In D. M. Boje, B. Burnes and J. Hassard (Eds.), *The Routledge Companion to Organizational Change*. (pp. 580–597). London and New York: Routledge.

Bourdieu, P. (1989). Social space and symbolic power. *Sociological Theory*, 7(1), 14–25.

Bourdieu, P. (1993). *Sociology in Question*. London: Sage Publications.

Bourdieu, P. (1996). *The State Nobility*. (Translated: Lauretta C. Clough). Cambridge, MA: Polity Press.

Bourdieu, P. and L. Wacquant (1992). *An Invitation to Reflexive Sociology*. Chicago, IL and London: University of Chicago Press.

Bovey, W. H. and A. Hede (2001). Resistance to organizational change: The role of defense mechanisms. *Journal of Managerial Psychology*, 16(7), 534–548.

Boyd, N. M. and D. S. Bright (2007). Appreciative inquiry as a mode of action research for community psychology. *Journal of Community Psychology*, 35(8), 1019–1036.

Bradford, D. L. and J. I. Porras (2005). A historical view of the future of OD: An interview with Jerry I. Porras. In D. L. Bradford and W. W. Burke (Eds.), *Reinventing Organization Development: New Approaches to Change in Organizations*. (pp. 43–64). San Francisco, CA: Pfeiffer.

Buchanan, D. and D. Boddy (1992). *The Expertise of the Change Agent: Public Performance and Backstage Activity*. Reading, MA: Prentice Hall.

Burnes, B. (2015). Understanding resistance to change: Building on Coch and French. *Journal of Change Management*, 15(2), 92–116.

Coghlan, D. (1993). A person-centered approach to dealing with resistance to change. *Leadership & Organization Development Journal*, 14(4), 10–14.

Dent, E. B. and S. G. Goldberg (1999). Challenging "Resistance to Change". *The Journal of Applied Behavioral Science*, 35(1). 25–41.

Fincham, R. and T. Clark (2002). Introduction: The emergence of critical perspective on consulting. In T. Clark and R. Fincham (Eds.), *Critical Consulting: New Perspectives on the Management Advice Industry*. (pp. 1–18). Oxford: Blackwell.

Ford, J. D. and L. W. Ford (2009). Decoding resistance to change. *Harvard Business Review*, 87(4), 99–103.

Ford, J. D. and L. W. Ford (2010). Stop blaming resistance to change and start using it. *Organizational Dynamics*, 39(1), 24–36.

Ford, J. D., L. W. Ford and A. D'Amelio (2008). Resistance to change: The rest of the story. *The Academy of Management Review*, 33(2), 362–377.

French, W. L. and C. H. Bell Jr. (1999). *Organization Development: Behavioral Science Interventions for Organization Improvement*. Norwood, NJ: Prentice Hall.

Gergen, K. J., M. M. Gergen and J. F. Barrett (2004). 'Dialogue: Life and death of the organization'. In D. Grant, C. Hardy, C. Oswick, N. Philips and L. Putnam (Eds.), *Handbook of Organization Discourse*. Thousand Oaks, CA: Sage Publications. Retrieved from www.swarthmore.edu/sites/default/files/assets/documents/kenneth--gergen/Dialogue_Life_and_Death_of_the_Organization.pdf

Herman, S. M. (1990). Lost in the system. *Organization Development Journal*, 8(1), 13–19.

Hon, A. H., M. Bloom and J. M. Crant (2014). Overcoming resistance to change and enhancing creative performance. *Journal of Management*, 40(3), 919–941.

Illouz, E. (2007). *Cold Intimacies: The Making of Emotional Capitalism*. London: Polity Press.

Jansen, K. J. (2000). The emerging dynamics of change: Resistance, readiness, and momentum. *People and Strategy*, 23(2), 53.

Kotter, J. P. (1990). *A Force for Change: How Leadership Differs from Management*. New York: The Free Press.

Kotter, J. P. (1995). Leading change: Why transformation efforts fail. *Harvard Business Review*, 73(2), 59–67.

Kotter, J. P. and L. A. Schlesinger (2008). Choosing strategies for change. *Harvard Business Review*, 86(7/8), 130.

Lahire, B. (2002). How to keep a critical tradition alive: A tribute to Pierre Bourdieu. *Review of International Political Economy*, 9(4), 595–600.

Lizardo, O. (2004). The cognitive origins of Bourdieu's habitus. *Journal for the Theory of Social Behaviour*, 34(4), 375–401.

Michel, A., R. Todnem By and B. Burnes (2013). The limitations of dispositional resistance in relation to organizational change. *Management Decision*, 51(4), 761–780.

Nord, W. R. and J. M. Jermier (1994). Overcoming resistance to resistance: Insights from a study of the shadows. *Public Administration Quarterly*, 17(4), 396–409.

Oreg, S. (2003). Resistance to change: Developing an individual differences measure. *Journal of Applied Psychology*, 88(4), 680.

Oreg, S. (2006). Personality, context, and resistance to organizational change. *European Journal of Work and Organizational Psychology*, 15(1), 73–101.

Oreg, S., M. Vakola and A. Armenakis (2011). Change recipients' reactions to organizational change: A 60-year review of quantitative studies. *The Journal of Applied Behavioral Science*, 47(4), 461–524.

Peters, J. T. and R. H. Waterman (1982). *In Search of Excellence*. New York: Harper and Row.

Piderit, S. K. (2000). Rethinking resistance and recognizing ambivalence: A multidimensional view of attitudes toward an organizational change. *Academy of Management Review*, 25(4), 783–794.

Ritzer, G. (2000). *Modern Sociological Theory*. Boston, MA: McGraw-Hill Education.

Schein, E. H. (1987). *Process Consulting: Lessons for Managers and Consultants*. (Vol. 2). Reading, MA: Addison-Wesley.

Schein, E. H. (1991). *Process Consulting Revisited: Building the Helping Relationships*. Reading, MA: Addison-Wesley, OD Series.

Schein, E. H. (1996). Kurt Lewin's change theory in the field and in the classroom: Notes toward a model of managed learning. *Systems Practice*, 9(1), 27–47.

Schein, E. H. (2000). The next frontier: Edgar Schein on organizational therapy. interview by Quick, C. J. with Gavin, H. J. *The Academy of Management Executive*, 14(1), 31–48.

Schein, E. H. (2005). Organization development: A wedding of anthropology and Organization therapy. In D. L. Bradford and W. W. Burke (Eds.), *Reinventing Organization Development: New Approaches to Change in Organizations.* (pp. 131–144). San Francisco, CA: Pfeiffer.

Schein, E. H. (2010). *Organizational Culture and Leadership*. San Francisco, CA: Jossey-Bass.

Scott, C. D. and D. T. Jaffe (1988). Survive and thrive in times of change. *Training & Development Journal*, 42(4), 25–28.

Senge, P. (1990). *The Fifth Discipline: The Art and Science of the Learning Organization*. New York: Currency Doubleday.

Shimoni, B. (2017). What is resistance to change? *Academy of Management Perspectives*, 31(4), 257–270.

Spreitzer, G. M. and R. E. Quinn (1996). Empowering middle managers to be transformational leaders. *The Journal of Applied Behavioral Science*, 32(3), 237–261.

Voronov, M. and W. P. Woodworth (2012). OD discourse and domination. In D. M. Boje, B. Burnes and J. Hassard (Eds.), *The Routledge Companion to Organizational Change.* (pp. 440–455). London and New York: Routledge.

Waddell, D. and A. S. Sohal (1998). Resistance: A constructive tool for change management. *Management Decision*, 36(8), 543–548.

Zander, A. (1950). Resistance to change: Its analysis and prevention. *Advanced Management Journal*, 4(5), 9–11.

6 HOOD in Action

The Chapter's Argument and Goal

In this chapter,[1] I use my consulting experience in a surgery department of a big hospital in Israel to exemplify how HOOD works in practice. Prof. Needle, the head of the department, invited me to help the department solve its intense conflictual interactions. According to Prof. Needle and the great majority of the department's members, the conflictual interactions, which prevented almost any possible effective communication, were the result of Dr. Goldberg's "stubborn personality" and disruptive and aggressive communication style. Dr. Goldberg was a significant member of the department. My role, as defined by Prof. Needle, was to help the department develop better interpersonal communication among its members and especially with Dr. Goldberg.

Interviews with all the department members (physicians, nurses and social workers) showed that Dr. Goldberg's daily interactions with others were indeed very aggressive. Her behavior reflected deep hostility, very often in the form of public insults and humiliating comments. At the same time, the interviews indicated that Dr. Goldberg's behavior was part of a bigger social picture reflecting a history of argumentative struggles in the department.

These struggles, I found, started years ago, mainly among Prof. Needle, the head of the department, and a group of three important veteran physicians, whom I defined as the "founding generation". The founding generation, (two male and one female physician) were caught in nostalgia for a magic past in which, they frequently mentioned, they and the former head ran the department in an affirmative social reality defined by sharing and collaboration. This nostalgia did not give any opportunity to new ideas suggested by Prof. Needle. Prof. Needle in turn kept the members of the founding generation far from the department's leadership and decision-making center. By doing that, he helped maintain both the founding generation's attachment to the past and their attempts to recreate that past by getting rid of Dr. Goldberg.

From the interviews, then, I learned that understanding Dr. Goldberg's struggling behavior entailed focusing not only on her psychological dispositions ("stubborn personality"), as people in the department understood this behavior, but also, perhaps mainly, on the conflictual interactions and power struggles of the whole department especially among the department's powerful agents. These power struggles, produced among the departments' members, including Dr. Goldberg, a shared habitus (social dispositions) organized around contesting values and norms expressed by aggressive patterns of communication.

The understanding of Dr. Goldberg's (and the rest of the department members') disruptive behavior not necessarily as a product of psychological dispositions but of social dispositions derived from the department's constant power struggles defines this chapter's goal and theoretical contribution. The goal of the chapter is to show how HOOD theoretically and practically understands and copes with organization problems and change.

Case Study: The Surgery Department

Prof. Needle invited me to solve the department's problem of intense conflictual interactions. The conflictual interactions, according to Prof. Needle and others in the department, were the result of Dr. Goldberg's "stubborn personality" and aggressive behavior. One of the department's senior physicians said, "She causes competition and jealousy".

Dr. Goldberg's interactions with others in the department were indeed very aggressive. Approaching one of the department's nurses, Dr. Goldberg says: "I did not study medicine only to wait for an available nurse". In my visits at the department, though, I realized that Dr. Goldberg's behavior was only one example of the struggles in the department. As part of these struggles, Prof. Needle, the head of the department, communicates with participants in a one-sided and very centralized way promoting and devaluing people using concealed and inconsistent criteria. According to one of the department's senior physicians:

> He consults but always does the opposite . . . [H]e is very centralized.

> Prof. Needle use to say I hear you but I am the head of the department and I decide.

> There was a committee but he decided alone.

The interviews indicated, however, that most of the participants engaged intensively in very disruptive behavior. Aggressive and hostile letters sent and filed at the Human Resource department, violent ways of talking and personal boycotts are only a few examples. "[We] are like a sick person who sees everything as an extreme", said the department's senior social worker.

The interviews also showed that this disruptive situation started about 10 years earlier between Prof. Needle and the "founding generation", a small but very dominant group of three physicians. Trapped by sentimental feelings about the past, they continually talked about the advantages of the former department head. They kept talking about the creative and enabling climate he created. One of the three said:

> [W]we were proud. We loved to come . . . fun to work . . . we were a team.

Talking about the past was always in contrast with the present time and with Prof. Needles' poor management, as we can see in the following quotation from another member of the founding generation:

> I blame him for his decision to give tenure to Dr. Goldberg.

The founding generation very often conducted meetings in private houses (with other physicians, nurses and social workers) aimed at finding ways to get rid of Dr. Goldberg and to make Prof. Needle more cooperative. Prof. Needle, in his turn, as the participants repeatedly said, could not find the leadership necessary to establish a new reality that would give the founding generation (and other participants) appropriate work conditions (participation, sharing and cooperation) that could bring back their sense of belonging and satisfaction. One of the founding generation said:

> Prof. Needle is very formal . . . [he] does not care about teamwork . . . [he] does not care how people feel.

Dr. Goldberg's aggressive behavior, then, was largely a reflection of disruptive interactions and power struggles of the whole department in which, as described by a senior physician,

> [E]every day [we have] a new war . . . People get positions only through manipulations.

Another physician:

> People try to turf (said in English) each other, to control.

Dr. Goldberg in a letter to one of the veteran physicians:

> [Y]you are using violent language toward a doctor . . . I am shocked
> I got your hate letter.

Dr. Goldberg in the interview with me:

> They want to eliminate me!

HOOD: Problem Solving and Change

Prof. Needle and the majority of the participants defined the department's problem in psychological terms. For them, the department's intensive conflictual interactions were mainly the result of Dr. Goldberg's "stubborn personality" and aggressive behavior. On the contrary, I claim that Dr. Goldberg's aggressive behavior was not necessarily a result of psychological dispositions. Rather, it was generated primarily by her habitus, the social dispositions she adopted from the department's stormy social structure (a competitive worldview, complete lack of tolerance of the needs of others and significantly asymmetric power relations). This was produced and reproduced constantly mainly by struggles among the agents in power, the founding generation and the head of the department. Examples are the hostile letters and violent language used by the founding generation, and a one-sided communication and non-transparent promotion processes used by the head of the department.

With this in mind, I assert that understanding social agents' behavior requires us "first to understand the field with which and against which" it has been formed (Bourdieu, 2007, p. 4). Indeed, the more I learned about the struggles in the department, the less I saw Dr. Goldberg's aggressive behavior as a psychological construct, a construct in which a single person (Dr. Goldberg), isolated from the social structure, simply did not have the personal skills needed to approach other people effectively. Instead, Dr. Goldberg's resistance was dynamically formed with and against the department's conflicted social life.

As Bourdieu's (1993, p. 82) theory of practice asserts, social interactions are not separated from the wider social context in which they take place. What happens between two persons or between two groups is always connected, organized and mastered by the objective relations and language accepted in the wider groups to which the two belong. Dr. Goldberg's aggressive interactions with other participants, from this perspective, reflect the two dominant groups in the surgery department (the founding generation and the head of the department) and their competition and constant struggles over resources, control and positions (Bourdieu and Wacquant, 1992, p. 97). I believe that an inspection focused only on Dr. Goldberg's interactions with others would not have noticed that these interactions reflected the entire set of relationships in the department's social field, especially the significant competitive relations between the founding generation and the head of the department (Forson, Özbilgin, Ozturk, and Tatli, 2014).

Following Bourdieu (1989), I claim that people are not socially passive. Because social structures become part of their habitus (social dispositions), they also control the way they apply social structures—they not only reproduce and perform, but also produce and innovate, the social structure. Specifically, Dr. Goldberg was not a powerless agent who simply applied the department's stormy social structure against her will. By confronting other participants in a very aggressive and insulting style and by openly challenging other physicians' expertise, she creatively refined and 'improved' her habitus and hostile behavior that in turn contributed to the production of the department's combative social structure.

Applying HOOD, then, helped me to understand that an the complexity of the department's social life. That is, to see that the department's disruptive interactions, including those practiced by Dr. Goldberg, were a product of the dialectical relations between Dr. Goldberg's aggressive behavior and the department's troubled social structure, produced and diffused mainly by the founding generation and the head of the department. I can only guess that Prof. Needle, like the rest of the participants (and perhaps like many others in the individualistic modern western world), assumed that if Dr. Goldberg only properly 'work' on herself, the department would also change.

Effective organizational problem solving and change from the HOOD perspective, then, involves improving consultees' reflexivity to structures and behavior. In the surgery department, this would include an understanding of the relationships between a competitive worldview, a zero tolerance for the needs of others, asymmetric power relations with a one-sided communication style by the head of the department, hostile letters sent to and filed at the Human Resource department, violent language and personal boycotts by the members of the department.

When the concept of habitus is at the center of the problem-solving process, HOOD responds to researchers in the 1970s and 80s who demonstrated the need to develop theoretical and practical ways to overcome the dichotomy between individual and structure in processes of organizational change (Friedlander and Brown, 1974). In the surgery department, the concept of habitus enabled me to overcome that dichotomy by changing the personal behavior of the powerful agents—the founding generation, the head of the department and Dr. Goldberg—thereby changing the social structure produced by their behavior. Indeed, the focus on habitus encouraged the founding generation and the head of the department to take responsibility for creating the intensive struggles in the department and for their future change. They both agreed that they were probably mainly responsible for the production of social structure (conflictual culture, worldview, schema of thinking and practical knowledge) that in the form of personal habitus generated an aggressive communication style among the department's members, including Dr. Goldberg.

Note

1 The chapter is based on Shimoni (2018).

Bibliography

Bourdieu, P. (1989). Social space and symbolic power. *Sociological Theory*, 7(1), 14–25.
Bourdieu, P. (1993). *Sociology in Question*. London: Sage Publications.
Bourdieu, P. (2007). *Sketch for a Self-Analysis*. Cambridge, MA: Polity Press.
Bourdieu, P. and L. Wacquant (1992). *An Invitation to Reflexive Sociology*. Chicago, IL and London: University of Chicago Press.
Forson, C., M. Özbilgin, M. B. Ozturk and A. Tatli (2014). Multi-level approaches to entrepreneurship and small business research: Transcending dichotomies with Bourdieu. In E. Chell and M. Karatas-Ozkan (Eds.), *Handbook of Research on Small Business and Entrepreneurship*. (pp. 54–69). Cheltenham: Edward Elgar Publishing.
Friedlander, F. and L. D. Brown (1974). Organization development. *Annual Review of Psychology*, 25(1), 313–341.
Illouz, E. (2007). *Cold Intimacies: The Making of Emotional Capitalism*. London: Polity Press.
Rose, N. (1991). Experts of the soul. *Psychologie und Geschichte*, 91–99. Retrieved from http://journals.zpid.de/index.php/PuG/article/viewFile/103/142
Shimoni, B. (2018). Bringing agency and social structure back into organization development: Toward a practice of habitus consulting. *Journal of Applied Behavioral Science*, 54(2), 208–225.

7 HOOD's Objectives in OD Change Processes

The organizing assumption of this chapter is that if the habitus is central in the work of social production, that is, in generating new worldviews and practices, any change initiative must begin with exploring and transforming people's habitus. "In order to change the world", as Bourdieu says, "we must change the world-making, that is, the worldview and the practical performance through which groups are produced and recreated" (Bourdieu, 1989, p. 23).

Habitus and Social Continuity

Before we celebrate the discovery that working on the habitus is the place to start changing processes of social production, it is necessary to briefly review assertions that the habitus participates in conservation and social reproduction rather than change. According to these assertions, because the habitus is the internalization of the social structure that belongs to a specific field, its performance is limited to the logic of this field, to its doxa and taken-for-granted language and behavior. Social agents from this perspective do not have interpretive space. They move only inside the boundaries put by their capital and position in the social field in which they operate (Raedeke, Green, Hodge, and Valdivia, 2003).

These critiques posit, then, that in Bourdieu's vision individuals are socially passive agents who are pulled and pushed into various actions and positions in life by structural forces. Thus, there is no scope for individual choice or possibilities of individual emancipation from circumstances. Frederic Vandenberghe (1999; Quoted also by Özbilgin, Tatli, and Queen, 2005, p. 864) suggests that Bourdieu "should open up his system, avoid deterministic descriptions of stable reproduction, and give voluntarism its due".

Bourdieu himself admits that the habitus tends to reproduce itself and the social structure in which it produced and operates. Specifically, the habitus, which stems from the primary socialization, becomes the social agent's "second nature" and thus reproduces itself and the actions that are consistent with the social conditions in which it was produced in the past (Emirbayer and Williams, 2005, p. 694). In this context, Bourdieu speaks of a reality in which people tend to prefer experiences and behaviors that support the habitus they hold in order to protect themselves from situations of uncertainty or crisis, situations in which their habitus dispositions are incompatible with those of the existing social field. In other words, people prefer to participate in interpersonal interactions and social groups where their social dispositions can express themselves freely and are accepted by others. Participation in these groups enables them to reproduce the group's existing reality and reaffirm the vitality of their own habitus.

Habitus and Social Change

The habitus, then, is "a matrix of perceptions, appropriation and actions" (Bourdieu, 1977, p. 95), derived from the field's social structure. However, Bourdieu argues that despite the consistent, stable, durable nature of this matrix, the habitus is flexible and adaptable and thus is able to adjust to other social contexts by adopting new social dispositions. "The habitus is an abstract, non-context specific, transposable matrix" (Lizardo, 2004, p. 392). Participants in organizations, for example, adopt the organization's habitus, which Bourdieu defines as "specific habitus", that is sometimes different from the habitus they acquired in early socialization (Emirbayer and Williams, 2005, p. 694). "For sure", says Frederic Vandenberghe (1999, p. 50) in his epistemological analysis of Bourdieu's work, "the habitus is the product of the social structures, but if one stops there, one falls into the trap of pure determinist reading and forgets that, as the generative principle of actions, evaluations, and perceptions, the habitus also structures the social world".

Specifically, people do not behave in a way that automatically responds to dispositions given by the field's social structure but also in a way that is influenced by their personal experience (Leander, 2001). They possess capitals and occupy positions and they develop strategies to preserve or change the field's existing capitals and positions. Bourdieu says (Bourdieu and Wacquant, 1992, pp. 108–109),

> Social agents are not "particles" that are mechanically pushed and pulled by external forces. They are rather bearers of capitals, and depending on their trajectory and on the position they occupy in the field by virtue of their endowment (volume and structure) in capital, they have a propensity to orient themselves actively either toward the preservation of the distribution of capital or toward the subversion of this distribution.

People [then] have choices, make strategies, and try to mobilize whatever power they have in their relations to others, as Bourdieu shows in his book *Social Structures of the Economy*, using the case of real estate agents that use a variety of strategies to "impose themselves on the buyers" (Leander, 2001. p. 348).

The habitus thus embodies a deterministic structure that dictates action but leaves room for creativity, inventions and improvisations (Sewell, 1992). In his research into Bourdieu's cognitive origins, Omar Lizardo (2004, p. 380) says that "Bourdieu remained a structuralist throughout, but his notion of structuralism was modified through the introduction of concerns regarding the genesis and the historical development of structure" in a given social field. Thus, as a structured space, the social field for Bourdieu "tends to structure the habitus, while the habitus tends to structure the perceptions of the field" (quoted by Everett, 2002, p. 65). Bourdieu presents this idea of the habitus as a socially and historically constructed entity in an interview with political activist Kevin Ovenden (Bourdieu, 2000, p. 3) on resistance and anti-capitalism:

> I was not a structuralist . . . I developed the concept of "habitus" to incorporate the objective structures of society and the subjective role of agents within it . . . [T]he habitus is a set of dispositions, reflexes and forms of behavior people acquire through action in society, for example, whether they are brought up in a middle class environment or in working class suburbs . . . [In other words, the habitus] is part of how society reproduces itself. But there is also a change . . . People can find that their expectations and way of living are suddenly out of step with the new social position they find themselves in.

For Bourdieu, then, understanding the concept of habitus presents an opportunity for personal and social change, for creating new thought and behaviors and for expressing expectations and a new way of life. People act within a structural framework that limits them, but they have control over the way they understand and implement this structural framework. They know what the right things to do are in given circumstances, which strategies they should employ in accordance with the situation in which they operate, and what power they should recruit or mobilize in their relationships with others (Leander, 2001). They improve their cultural and economic capitals by acquiring education and political capital and by participating in social movements that engage in social change in which they are interested.

The habitus dispositions, then, are durable and they tend to reproduce themselves, but they are not perpetual. They are dynamic in nature, adjustable, renewable and changeable. In Bourdieu's words (quoted by Garrett, 2007, p. 229), the habitus is:

> [N]ot something natural, inborn: being a product of history, that is of social experience and education, it may be changed by history,

that is by new experiences, education or training . . . Dispositions are long-lasting: they are tending to perpetuate, to reproduce themselves, but they are not eternal . . . Any dimension of habitus is very difficult to change but it may be changed through the process of awareness and of pedagogic effort.

HOOD's Objectives

In what follows, I present HOOD's objectives in processes of change and development. In order to do that, I invite the readers to think of themselves as HOOD consultants taking part in a personal or a group "pedagogic effort" aiming to develop consultees' reflexivity to their habitus. Consultees are asked to think about their own social dispositions (habitus) and search for the reflection of these dispositions in their behavior and in "the interplay between capital, fields and habitus, which exist in interdependency and relationally with each other" (Tatli, Özbilgin, and Karatas-Ozkan, 2015, p. 4). (See Table 7.1).[1]

Search for the Social Structure

Habitus-oriented OD encourages OD consultants to see individuals' thinking and behavior as a collective phenomenon (Swartz, 2002). That is, they are asked to understand individuals' behavior not only as a result of inner psychological dispositions but also of the social structure (shared thinking schemes, values and power relations) as it is demonstrated in the individual's habitus. From this perspective, I Understood Dr. Goldberg's disruptive behavior as not only a personal but also a social and collective phenomenon, a matter of the department's stormy social structure as reflected in her habitus (social dispositions).

Search for the Participants' Agency (and Not Only Self)

Habitus-oriented OD encourages OD consultants to help consultees recognize not only their personal self but also their agency. That is, HOOD

Table 7.1 The different objectives of OD and HOOD

OD	HOOD
Individuals' or groups' inner world	Social structure
Self	Agency
Psychological dispositions	Social dispositions
	Habitus
Interaction between subjective positions	Interaction between objective positions
Individuals and groups	Whole organization

encourages them to see the source of their behavior not only in their psychological dispositions (such as charisma, communication style and personal commitment), but also in their *agency*: their capital, resources and position in the organization's social structure. From this perspective, I understood Dr. Goldberg's aggressive behavior not only as an expression of her "problematic personality" but also, and perhaps mainly, as an expression of her weak agency. I claim that as a powerless agent with little social capital and marginal position in the department, an aggressive communication style was almost the only way for Dr. Goldberg to protect her needs and interests.

Search for the Habitus (Structure and Agency)

Helping consultees recognize the social structure in which they live and their agency is not enough. In addition, we want to help consultees recognize the dialectic relationship between the social structure and their agency in their habitus. Furthermore, a focus on the habitus grants consultees a view of both the influence of the social structure on the individuals' or groups' behavior and the influence of their behavior on the social structure. I believe that Dr. Goldberg's disruptive behavior was generated by the relationship between this specific behavior (disruptive) and the department's troubled social structure, which encouraged aggressive behaviors.

Search for the Relations Between Objective Positions

Habitus-oriented OD encourages OD consultants to see the organization's social reality not only as a network of subjective interpersonal relations (between selves) but also as a network of objective positions (between agents). In such a network, the (objective) specific behaviors do not express subjective interpersonal relations and inner motivations but rather objective positions derived from struggles for control and capital (Bourdieu and Wacquant, 1992, p. 97). For this reason I suggested that Prof. Needle not think of Dr. Goldberg's behavior only as an expression of her psychological dispositions (her "problematic personality", low personal commitment and inner disruptive motivations), but also, perhaps mainly, as a product of the social positions between Dr. Goldberg and others in the department, especially members of the founding generation. These asymmetric positions, I assumed, left Dr. Goldberg almost no option for communicating her opinion and desires except for disruptive behavior.

Search the Whole of the Organization

Using the concept of habitus as a starting point in OD processes enables consultants to focus not only on individuals' or groups' psychological dispositions, but also on the organization as a whole. As a site of interaction between individuals' behavior and the social structure, the habitus assumes wholeness and totality, since every social structure is embodied in and influenced by its wider social context. The focus on habitus (on the individuals' social dispositions adopted from the social structure) in the surgery department helped me understand the participants' disruptive behaviors, including Dr. Goldberg's, as partially a reflection, indeed a production, of the department's social structure.

HOOD in OD Practices

OD offers a varied set practices for self-development and growth including guided imagery, role-playing and open and unstructured dynamics. The aim of these practices is mainly to develop participants' consciousness of their psychological dispositions and awareness of their skills and abilities and their relations with others.

The HOOD fully adopts these practices. However, it uses these practices to develop participants' reflexivity to their habitus, social dispositions, and to the roots of these dispositions in the social structure, e.g., in power relations, control over capital and resources and position in the organization's social structure. The basic assumption is that identifying and changing participants' habitus is similar to identifying and changing the self, since over time both the habitus and the self become embedded in the individual's mind, emotions and body.

Tables 7.2 to 7.5 provide a framework for facilitating OD practices in the spirit of HOOD using four randomly selected subjects:

Table 7.2 Effective interpersonal communication

The workshop's organizing concept	Goal
Self	The goal of this workshop is to develop participants' reflexivity to their self and psychological dispositions. Developing this reflexivity serves as a point of departure for improving participants' listening skills, the way they deliver messages and their ability to reach compromise and agreement and thus apply more effective interpersonal communication.
Habitus	The goal of this workshop is to develop participants' reflexivity to their habitus and to the root of this habitus in the organization's social structure in which interactions take place and are constructed. Developing this reflexivity helps participants apply an effective interpersonal communication style that considers questions of power relations between groups to which each participant belongs, to the interests of these groups and their organizational goals.

Table 7.3 Organization culture

The workshop's organizing concept	Goal
Self	The goal of this workshop is to develop the participants' cultural reflexivity, e.g., awareness to the dominant culture (or cultures) in the organization and to the part this culture plays in constructing their thinking and behavior.
	Organizational culture in these workshops is a collective structure, a shared unconsciousness, that arises somewhere in the social space outside the individual and organizes thoughts and behavior.
Habitus	The goal of this workshop is to develop the participants' reflexivity to the presence of the organization culture in their habitus, or social dispositions.
	Organization culture in these workshops is a structure that from inside the participants, from their habitus, generates thoughts and behavior but is also constantly constructed and reconstructed by the participants, depending on their position in the organization's social structure.

Table 7.4 Leadership development

The workshop's organizing concept	Goal
Self	The goal of this workshop is to develop the participants' reflexivity to their psychological dispositions and to the impact of these dispositions on their leadership style; for instance, laissez-faire, autocratic and participative.
	The participants' reflexivity to their psychological dispositions and to their leadership style serve as a point of departure for the development of leadership skill such as effective communication and motivating employees.
Habitus	The goal of this workshop is to develop the participants' social reflexivity, e.g., awareness of the cultural, symbolic and social capitals that are specifically relevant for actualizing leadership in the organization's social field.
	The workshop focuses on the participants' capitals, and thus their position in the organization, as a point of departure for understanding the social and structural elements that they need to acquire in order to meet with cultural, symbolic and social capitals that are specifically relevant for actualizing leadership in their organization.

Table 7.5 Power and influence

The workshop's organizing concept	Goal
Self	The goal of this workshop is to develop the participants' political reflexivity and skills. That is, to develop their awareness of the dominant political struggles in the organization and the specific skills and strategies needed for managing these struggles. This workshop deals with power in its traditional form. That is, it aims to help the participants identify their own existing sources of power in Weberian terms (tradition, law or charisma) and use them to make others, a person or a group, act in the way they wish them to act.
Habitus	The goal of this workshop is to develop the participants' reflexivity to the unspoken aspects of power and influence in the organization and to processes of symbolic violence enacted by powerful agents in order to subtly reproduce the existing power structure. The workshop assumes that symbolic violence lies beyond, or below, the participants' consciousness and free will, and that its power and influence are usually experienced as something good, although ultimately it reproduces a social reality that is in contrast to the interests of those on which it is applied.

communication and interpersonal interaction, organizational culture, leadership development, and power and influence. The top of each table focuses on developing participants' consciousness of their self and psychological dispositions as a point of departure for improving their skills in the specific workshop subject; for instance, "effective interpersonal communication". The bottom part of each table focuses on achieving effective interpersonal communication by developing participants' reflexivity to their habitus and to social structure and conditions in which this habitus has been developed.

Needless to say, focusing on one of the two orientations, self or habitus, does not exclude the other. Each orientation has a different goal. A self-oriented OD uses these practices to search for the roots of behavior in the individual self and help participants to change their behavior. A habitus-oriented OD (HOOD) uses these practices to search for the roots of behavior in the social structure and help participants to change the social structure and the condition in which it has been developed.

Note

1 The development of the following section was inspired by Swartz (2002).

Bibliography

Bourdieu, P. (1977). *Outline of a Theory of Practice.* Cambridge, MA: Cambridge University Press.

Bourdieu, P. (1989). Social space and symbolic power. *Sociological Theory*, 7(1), 14–25.

Bourdieu, P. (2000). The politics of protest. An interview by Kevin Ovenden. *Socialist Review*, 242, 18–20.

Bourdieu, P. (2005). *The Social Structures of the Economy.* Cambridge, MA: Polity Press.

Bourdieu, P. and L. Wacquant (1992). *An Invitation to Reflexive Sociology.* Chicago, IL and London: University of Chicago Press.

Cassirer, E. (1972). *An Essay on Man* (1944). New Haven, CT: Yale University Press.

Emirbayer, M. V. and V. Johnson (2008). Bourdieu and organizational analysis. *Theory and Society*, 37(1), 1–44.

Emirbayer, M. and E. M. Williams (2005). Bourdieu and social work. *Social Service Review*, 79(4), 689–724, 690–694.

Everett, J. (2002). Organizational research and the praxeology of Pierre Bourdieu. *Organizational Research Methods*, 5(1), 56–80.

Garrett, P. M. (2007). Making social work more Bourdieusian: Why the social professions should critically engage with the work of Pierre Bourdieu. *Journal of Social Work*, 10(2), 225–243.

Leander, A. (2001). Review essay: Pierre Bourdieu on economics. *Review of International Political Economy*, 8(2), 344–353.

Lizardo, O. (2004). The cognitive origins of Bourdieu's habitus. *Journal for the Theory of Social Behavior*, 34(4), 375–401.

Özbilgin, M., A. Tatli and M. Queen (2005). Book review essay: 'Understanding Bourdieu's contribution to organization and management studies,' [Review of Outline of Theory of Practice; The Logic of Practice; Practical Reason: On the Theory of Action; An Invitation to Reflexive Sociology]. *The Academy of Management Review*, 30(4), 855–869.

Raedeke, A. H., J. J. Green, S. S. Hodge and C. Valdivia (2003). Farmers, the practice of farming and the future of agroforestry: An application of Bourdieu's concepts of field and habitus. *Rural Sociology*, 68(1), 64–86.

Sewell, Jr. W. H. (1992). A theory of structure: Duality, agency, and transformation. *American Journal of Sociology*, 98(1), 1–29.

Swartz, D. L. (2002). The sociology of habit: The perspective of Pierre Bourdieu. *The Occupational Therapy Journal of Research*, 22, 61s-69s.

Tatli, A., M. Özbilgin and M. Karatas-Ozkan (2015). Introduction: Management and organization studies meet Pierre Bourdieu. In A. Tatli, M. Özbilgin and M. Karatas-Ozkan (Eds.), *Pierre Bourdieu, Organization, and Management.* (pp. 1–18). London and New York: Routledge.

Vandenberghe, F. (1999). "The Real is Relational": An epistemological analysis of Pierre Bourdieu's generative structuralism. *Sociological Theory*, 17(1), 32–67.

8   Concluding Discussion

Overcoming the Personal-Social Dichotomy

As shown in chapter two, at least four discourses dominate the mainstream OD field. These four discourses differ in their perspectives on the source of consultees' thinking and behavior. The first discourse (1940s to 1950s), sees the source of thinking and behavior in the interaction between individuals and the social context (Lewin, 1939). The second (1960s), sees that interaction within the individual (Schein, 1999), the third (1970s to1980s), in the social context (Pettigrew, Thomas, and Whittington, 2001), and the fourth (1990s to current), in the interaction between individuals (Cooperrider and Srivastva, 1987). I claim that the deep logic organizing these discourses assumes the personal and the social as two separate entities and thus remains blind to the *combined* contribution of the two (the personal and the social) to the processes of producing and coping with organizational problems, change and development.

By considering equally the personal and the social and the dialectic relations between the two, HOOD, then, overcomes the personal-social dichotomy. Specifically, HOOD assumes that since every habitus (including the habitus of organizations' leaders) is part of wider social context, it (the habitus) transcends boundaries of body and role, departments, organizations and the field in which organizations are socially located. As we have seen, the focus on the habitus of Benny, John, Bill and Dr. Goldberg and on their social dispositions that embody the organization's social structure, enabled me to see the relative responsibility of both personal behavior and social structure. In all three cases, the so-called "problematic" behavior was a result of Kimono's and the surgery department's stormy social structure in which a specific (organizational) contested habitus developed.

Because of my focus on habitus I was able to go to the cognitive world of a vast range of consultees, a world in which the personal-social dichotomy does not exist, and search for the source of thinking and behavior in the social structure as integrated in habitus. Based on this experience, in this book I encourage OD consultants to keep polishing their mirrors that reflect consultees' personal thinking and behavior. However, these mirrors should not reflect only psychological but also *social* dispositions (habitus) that contain the organization's social structure, its practical knowledge, power relations and social positions.

Moral and Effective Consulting

Assuming habitus and social structure to be highly significant for understanding consultees' thoughts and behavior, in this book I argue that OD scholars and practitioners should unmask structural mechanisms that lie concealed behind the assumed social structures, e.g., accepted power relations and structures (allocation of resources and capitals), social positions, common cultural understandings, metaphors and practical knowledge.

Put another way, I claim that OD projects that refer to social structures as power-free and neutral that non-managerial consultees need to adapt to, and not as socially constructed mainly by those in power, are immoral and ineffective. They are immoral because they blame only non-managerial consultees for the production of organizational problems. They are ineffective since they ignore both the role of those in power in the construction of these problems and the perspectives of consultees in non-managerial positions for these specific problems.

Indeed, explicitly considering the significant role of the operation department's asymmetric power relations, exclusion and marginalization in producing Benny's (and others') habitus of not taking care of faults allowed me to both avoid the assumption that Benny is solely responsible for these faults and to consider his (Benny's) and others' perspectives on these specific faults. In John and Bill's case, considering the extreme battles among the two owner groups and the contested habitus these battles produced allowed me to see the owners' responsibility, not only John and Bill's, for the poor performance and to better understand John and Bill's destructive behavior. Explicitly referring to the conflicts among the surgery department's leaders as producers of the stormy social structure allowed me to see not only Dr. Goldberg but also the head of the department and the founding generation as responsible for the department's intense conflictual interactions and to understand better Dr. Goldberg's perspective on the department's intense conflictual interactions.

Criticizing Managerialism Is Not Anti-Manager

I believe that if I had responded directly to the contact person's expectations and focused solely on fixing the psychological dispositions of Benny, John, Bill and Dr. Goldberg (their personal commitment and communication skills and their so-called "stubborn personalities"), I would have performed a managerialist consultation. In a situation like this, I would have defined the change processes at Kimono and in the surgery department only in terms of those in power who invited my help.

The concept of habitus, which reflects the role of Kimono's and the surgery department's dominant agents in the production of the stormy social structure, helped me avoid a managerialist consulting approach. Specifically, the habitus allowed me to see the organizations' problems as subjected historically to social construction, power, control over capitals and social positions and thus to (jointly) conduct a change that considers the organizations' structural and not only individual level (as I was expected to do).

Bourdieu's critical theory, then, contributes to OD an approach that encourages consultants to develop consultees' reflexivity to habitus and to social structure. This approach has a great potential to help consultees uncover managerialist, non-neutral and self-interested practices enacted by those in power who control the organization's capitals and resources, knowledge and practice and define its dominating perspectives (Nathan and Whatley, 2006, pp. 65–66). At Kimono and in the surgery department, developing reflexivity to habitus and to social structure helped consultees (managers and non-managers) reflect critically upon management's oppressive practices and on the marginalizing social and political context, the contested and stormy social structures that through habitus generated the so-called problematic behaviors.

Deconstructing managerialism is not anti-manager. It does not aim to devalue managers' perspectives or undercut their power and positions. Instead, as shown in all three case studies, it aims to encourage reflecting on the organization's social complexity and help consultees act in a way that ultimately gives expression to perspectives of other than managers. Specifically, the habitus helps consider all participants as valuable sources of information about the organization's problems and about potential solutions for these problems—to create a more moral and effective organizational environment based on wide organizational knowledge and perspectives.

HOOD as a Bridge Between Organizations and Society

By putting habitus and social structure at the center of the consulting process, HOOD answers the calls who wish to see OD as a "progressive social movement" (Burnes and Cooke, 2012, p. 1417) that both responds to the demands of capitalism and exposes its often-invisible structural injustice. Specifically, the focus on habitus positions HOOD within OD's original role as a bridge between organizations and society (Martin, 2016) to help consultees maneuver more creatively and liberally within capitalist-oriented structures and injustice.

The exposure of capitalism's injustice does not mean OD should directly challenge macro-capitalist and neo-liberal structures. OD scholars and practitioners are not social activists, at least in my mind, and they should not take an active role in "macro-emancipation" (Alvesson and Willmott, 1992). Macro emancipation aims to change the labor market and society fundamentally, for instance their financial and employment policy and practice. That is, I do not expect HOOD to result in full equality of wages, in dramatic changes of managers' roles, in creating absolute democracy and in total elimination of job insecurity. Macro-emancipation is much larger than what I offer in this book and perhaps than what OD in its current form is able to achieve intellectually and practically. Furthermore, as noted, focusing on macro-emancipation has a potential to neglect limiting structures on the level of the organization such as managerial control and other marginalizing practices that exclude non-managerial perspectives from the center of the organization (Huault, Perret, and Spicer, 2014).

From its place between organizations and society, then, HOOD focuses on uncovering restrictive structures on the level of the organization. In order to do that, HOOD applies "micro-emancipation" that focuses on the creation of local and temporal "zones of freedom" (Huault, Perret, and Spicer, 2014, p. 41) in which the voice of non-manager consultees is heard and practically considered. Specifically, HOOD uses traditional OD therapeutic practices such as active listening and dynamic group workshops to develop consultees' reflexivity to habitus and social structure and thus to create emancipation from managers' oriented doxa—the taken-for-granted way of seeing the world. This emancipation, I believe, has the needed potential to help non-manager consultees participate in change and development processes as free as possible from oppressive structural burdens and bring their needs, interests and perspectives into the change process.

By liberating consultees' habitus from the organization's structural constrains, HOOD returns to OD's scholarly roots, which considered both the human and the pragmatic sides of organizations' change and development. It (HOOD) allows OD scholars and practitioners to write and apply an OD that is not only a set of techniques, aiming to help consultees effectively adapt to capitalism' structural demands. Rather, it offers a philosophy or attitude that from the place between organizations and society focuses "on the coupling of the humanistic change with meeting the organization's objectives" (Bennis, 1969; quoted by Voronov and Woodworth, 2012, p. 441).

Empowerment, Emancipation and Social Structure

Perhaps there are those who would say that democratic and participatory systems that are central to the field of OD, such as delegation of authority, autonomy and programs of personal empowerment (leadership development, self-management, active listening) are pure expression of emancipation (self-realization and liberation). Generally, they would ask why not turn the workplace into a site of self-expression and empowerment. Releasing personal potential, according to this line of thought, is not only effective, it can also turn organizations into better sites; sites of self-enrichment and development that serve employees in other spheres of life. A "grown" and "developed" employee, who can make decisions assertively, communicate effectively and motivate others in an emphatic way, they would say, will be a better friend and parent, a more creative community member and a good team player (Schein, 2009).

I completely agree with this. For me too, free self-expression, autonomy and empowerment are important. Applying them offers employees "more discretion over the work related activities, trusting them, and sharing more information with them" (Cunningham and Hyman, 1999; quoted by Voronov, 2005, p. 14). Yet practices like empowerment liberate employees only from their own self—from them*selves*. That is, they focus on emancipating the self from its own anger, frustration, low motivation and aggression, from psychological dispositions that generate ineffective behavior as defined by those in power, usually managers. In many respects, and as specifically Omer and Benny's case shows, empowerment represents an implicit regime of self-discipline and symbolic violence. It releases employees' full potential in order to realize goals set by managers and market. Largely, empowerment is a version of soft-capitalism, of a gentle way in which managers apply surveillance and get control (Costea, Crump, and Amiridis, 2008).

Empowerment, then, does not focus on restricting social structures and thus it is relatively limited in its effectiveness. Autonomy and independency are always within the boundaries of social structures such as practical knowledge, power relations, control over capitals and work processes, defined and managed by those in power and in accordance with profitability. As long as non-managerial consultees are not part of the design of these practices, in the good case these practices are only partially effective (Alvesson and Willmott, 1992) and in the worst case they reflect what Bourdieu (1990, p. 15) defines as "illusory freedoms". As David Boje and Grace Ann Rosile (2001, p. 93) tell us, the focus on processes such as empowerment is largely on generating the "feeling or belief that a person can direct the organization toward desired performance ends".

Emancipation for HOOD, then, does not end with empowerment, with democratic and participative systems, with active and emphatic listening or with self-expression enabled by the good spirit of those who control the organization's social structure and define it in terms of profitability and market. Rather, emancipation means developing consultees' reflexivity to habitus and thus to structural domination, coercion and marginalization. More specifically, *emancipation happens when non-managerial consultees develop reflexivity to habitus and social structure that shape and define specific ways of being and doing things, and use this reflexivity practically to express their perspectives and negotiate their positions and interests.* Equality in decision-making, participation in plans for organizing and *re*constructing working conditions and processes that involve exploitation, discrimination and exclusion, are just some of the practices on the way to emancipation. These practices, I believe, have the potential to increase the involvement of more participants in the organization's working dynamic and hence to create more just and effective change and development processes.

The Skills Required to Operate in Accordance With HOOD

HOOD requires consultants to adopt a dual perspective whose concepts and practices have their source in therapeutic psychology as adopted by OD, and in Pierre Bourdieu's theory of action. Acquiring therapeutic discourse and practices grants OD consultants the tools needed to create trustful relationships with consultees and develop consultees' responsibility for the organizational change process. The therapeutic tools that are brilliantly presented by Edgar Schein (1987, 1993, 2011) in his writing were highly significant in my interventions at Kimono and in the surgery department. Active listening and empathy helped me establish consulting relations grounded in trust and openness in spite of the struggles and deep interpersonal suspicions that dominated the social contexts in both workplaces.

Adopting Bourdieu's theory of action, especially the concepts of habitus, capital, field and symbolic violence, provides OD consultants with the theoretical framework needed to conduct action research or any other OD practice in a way that considers the organization's social field in complex and relational terms. This way considers equally and interconnectedly levels of behavior and structure. It allows consultants and consultees to see organizational problems as a result of dialectic interactions between human behavior, rooted in struggles for capitals and positions, and social structures such as power relations and practical knowledge.

Bibliography

Alvesson, M. and H. Willmott (1992). On the idea of emancipation in management and organization studies. *Academy of Management Review*, 17(3), 432–464.

Bennis, W. G. (1969). *Organization Development: Its Nature, Origins, and Prospects*. Reading, MA: Addison-Wesley.

Boje, D. M. and G. A. Rosile (2001). Where's the power in empowerment? Answers from Follett and Clegg. *The Journal of Applied Behavioral Science*, 37(1), 90–117.

Bourdieu, P. (1990). *In Other Words: Essays Towards a Reflexive Sociology*, tr. Matthew Adamson. Cambridge, MA: Polity Press in Association with Blackwell.

Burnes, B. and B. Cooke (2012). Review article: The past, present and future of organization development: Taking the long view. *Human Relations*, 65(11), 1395–1429.

Cooperrider, D. L. and S. Srivastva (1987). Appreciative inquiry in organizational life. In W. A. Pasmore and R. Woodman (Eds.), *Research in Organizational Change and Development*. (pp. 129–169). Greenwich, CT: JAI Press.

Costea, B., N. Crump and K. Amiridis (2008). Managerialism, the therapeutic habitus and the self in contemporary organizing. *Human Relations*, 61(5), 661–685.

Cunningham, I. and J. Hyman (1999). The poverty of empowerment? A critical case study. *Personnel Review*, 28(3), 192–207.

Huault, I., V. Perret and A. Spicer (2014). Beyond macro-and micro-emancipation: Rethinking emancipation in organization studies. *Organization*, 21(1), 22–49.

Jermier, J. M. (1998). Introduction: Critical perspective on organizational control. *Administrative Science Quarterly*, 43(2), 235–256.

Lewin, K. (1939). Field theory and experiment in social psychology: Concepts and methods. *American Journal of Sociology*, (1), 868–896.

Martin, M. (2016). Taking OD back to the future. *Organization Development Journal*, 34(2), 61.

Nathan, J. D. and A. Whatley (2006). Critical theory: A means for transforming organization development. *Organization Development Journal*, 24(2).

Pettigrew, A., M. Thomas and R. Whittington (Eds.) (2001). *Handbook of Strategy and Management*. London: Sage Publications.

Schein, E. H. (1987). *Process Consultation: Lessons for Managers and Consultants*. (Vol. 2). Reading, MA: Addison-Wesley.

Schein, E. H. (1993). On dialogue, culture and organizational learning. *Reflections*, 4(4), 27–38.

Schein, E. H. (1999). *Process Consultation Revisited: Building the Helping Relationship*. Reading, MA: Addison-Wesley.

Schein, E. H. (2009). *Helping: How to Offer, Give, and Receive Help*. San Francisco, CA: BK.

Voronov, M. (2005). Should critical management studies and organization development collaborate? Invitation to a contemplation. *Organization Management Journal*, 2(1), 4–26.

Voronov, M. and W. P. Woodworth (2012). OD discourse and domination. In D. M. Boje, B. Burnes and J. Hassard (Eds.), *The Routledge Companion to Organizational Change*. (pp. 440–455). London and New York: Routledge.

9 Summary and Future Research

Why *Habitus*-Oriented OD and Not *Self*-Oriented OD?

The dominance of the individualistic orientation in Western social structure, in the modern labor market and specifically in individually oriented OD, is the point of departure of this book. Following other writers, I say that the individualistic orientation's basic assumption in which the individual self is *the* most significant 'tool' managers and organizations should constantly develop misses the opportunity to consider the organization's social and structural conditions (Costea, Crump, and Amiridis, 2008; De Vos, 2010; Gergen and Thatchenkery, 1996; Illouz, 2008; Voronov and Woodworth, 2012).

Specifically, the organizing principle of this book is that the concept of habitus, which stands for not psychological but social dispositions adopted from wider social contexts, enables OD scholars and practitioners to go beyond the individual self. It enables us to work on the macro level of the organization in a way that sees thoughts and behaviors as a result of objective and material aspects of the organization such as control over capitals, power relations and positions. As we have seen, using the concept of habitus focused the change process at Kimono and at the surgery department both on understanding the roots of participants' thoughts and behavior in the organizations' social structure and on changing the social conditions in which this social structure has developed.

I suspect that some readers will think that the concept of habitus, like the concept of self, with its intangible *cognitive* nature, is naïve or detached from the organization's 'real' life and thus cannot capture objective and material aspects of the organization. Such an argument would say that not everything is in the mind of the organization members, in their internal social dispositions or habitus. It is impossible to deny the existence of objective and visible structural reality. For example, when writers propose to change the "work itself", they mean physical changes in the way the work is organized: a *real* change in measurable job characteristics such as delegation of authority, responsibility and autonomy, diversity of work, definition of roles, work processes and organization structure (Beer, Eisenstat, and Spector, 1990; Hackman and Oldham, 1976). All these are not only in peoples' heads (habitus)—they are objective and material matters that are not inside but outside, they are not a subjective but an objective reality seen by everyone.

This is true, but only partially. Mechanical and administrative control of work, like the organization's structure, for instance, is indeed permanent and durable. However, this durability does not mean the organization's structure is 'natural' or has an internal logic of its own. Instead, the organization's structure is constructed and reconstructed in constant negotiations between social structures and individuals' behavior through power struggles over symbolic and material capitals and positions (Battilana, 2006; Deetz, 1992). The objective status of what we often call "formal" organization structure, then, is largely a product of historical social construction and power-struggles embedded in habitus. Through the habitus, the constructed and objectified organization structure in turn generates the social reality in organizations and enforces its form and content on the organization members. As Bourdieu (1977, p. 91) says,

> The objective universe is made up of objects which are the product of objectifying operations structured according to the very structures which the mind applies to it. The mind is a metaphor of the world of objects which is itself but an endless circle of mutually reflecting metaphors.

The habitus, then, is about consultants helping their consultees identify whether they want to generate fundamental structural change that considers the objective and material sides of organizations.

Why *Habitus*-Oriented OD and Not *Culture*-Oriented OD?

I assume that at least some readers wonder why I am using the concept of habitus and not the concept of culture. OD writers, they would say, have already developed a holistic structural approach that uses the concept of culture to understand and motivate individuals' and groups' viewpoints, identities and behaviors. I claim that while both culture and habitus generate thinking, emotions and behaviors (Hurtado, 2009), culture as a "coercive background structure" (Schein, 2010, p. 3) and habitus as a "structuring structure" (Bourdieu, 1989, p. 18), they differ in at least two aspects that are relevant for understanding why I use the concept of habitus.

First, mainstream OD generally does not consider the concept of culture in terms of social construction. It views cultures largely as static, stable and rigid entities with an independent existence. Cultures from this perspectives shape or control (Ray, 1986) individuals' and groups' emotions, perspectives and behaviors, what is often defined as a symbolic management approach (Alvesson, 1995). This instrumental approach to culture, then, sees the personal and the cultural as two separated entities in which the cultural engineers consultees' ways of thinking and patterns of behaviors (Kunda, 1992).

There is one exception. When it comes to managers, mainstream OD does consider social constructions. That is, social constructions happen mainly at the level of managers who are the producers of cultures. Non-managerial consultees are required to accept these constructions and see them as taken-for-granted maps showing them the right way to think, feel and behave (Alvesson and Willmott, 1992; Schein, 1987). Without revealing the principles and forces behind cultural production, such as control over capitals, positions and power relations, culture for mainstream OD implicitly serves non-managerial consultees as a 'natural' source of knowledge and practice.

Mainstream OD is thus strongly committed to structure (in terms of culture) and less to social construction. The concept of habitus, in contrast, is *fully* committed to social construction. As we have seen, every habitus, including the habitus of organizations' leaders, is embedded in and subjected to social construction influenced by wider social forces. Habitus exceeds the boundaries of the individual body, roles and organizations. It chooses a "third way" which considers the role of powerful and powerless agents in the construction of knowledge (Özbilgin, Tatli, and Queen, 2005, p. 856). Specifically, non-managerial consultees for habitus-oriented OD (HOOD) are not only reproducing (applying) but also producing (changing) the organization's social reality (Sewell, 1992). As producers of social reality, they are an unseparated part of the organization's social structure and thus should *reflect* its opportunities and constraints and their own and others' part in the production of this structure.

For HOOD, then, non-managerial consultees are not psychological subjects that consultants should adapt to the social structure. Instead, they are sociological agents who actively take part in the construction of the organization's social structure—agents "who are socially constructed as active and acting in the field under consideration by the fact that they possess the necessary properties to be effective, to produce effects, in this field" (Bourdieu and Wacquant, 1992, pp. 107–108).

A second way in which the concepts of habitus and culture (as represented by mainstream OD) differ is in the way they relate to the organization's symbolic, objective and materialist properties. The concept of culture largely refers only to the organization's symbolic properties such as norms, values and metaphors (Alvesson, 2002). The concept of habitus refers to the symbolic as well, but as we have seen, also to the objective and material aspects of the organization and thus grants OD consultants "a potential to shed light onto the material and symbolic resources that shape organizational life" (Tatli, Özbilgin, and Karatas-Ozkan, 2015, pp. 8–9).

Criticism and the Duty to Offer an Alternative Practical Approach

The intensive use of the individually oriented perspective in mainstream OD (defined here as *individually oriented OD*) has been criticized in this book and in much other research (for instance, Voronov and Woodworth, 2012). Nevertheless, following the theoretical stance of this book, which considers social structures as central in shaping individuals' mind and practice, I do not aim my criticism exclusively at specific OD scholars or consultants. Individually oriented OD is part of a tradition. It represents the humanist perspective of the 1960s that developed in response to structural ideas of Taylorism. The Taylorist engineers, says Edgar Schein (1969), overlooked the individual person or treated him and her as part of the structure. As a response, OD scholars and practitioners devoted their research and consulting careers to the development of a consulting approach that positions the individual at the center of the consulting process and defines her and him as the most significant target of change and development processes.

In this book I do not limit myself to criticism but I offer an alternative approach, the HOOD. Criticism alone can produce an abstract theoretical discussion whose values and meanings are nonconcrete, disconnected from the research field and aimless—i.e., not fulfilling the responsibility of the critic to offer alternative views (Grenfell, 2010; Lahire, 2002). Writing critically, I believe, is an important step in improving existing theoretical and practical knowledge. Like Andre Spicer and Charlotta Levay, 2012), I also claim that criticism without solutions risks creating negative images of the OD field—without offering an alternative, this criticism is absent and problematic. If we fail to offer solutions, such criticism is merely an abstraction.

Furthermore, critical writing that focuses only on the 'problematic' without offering an alternative has the potential to perpetuate existing models, which are the objects of the critic. Such writing would contribute to the production of texts that, while considering deeply problems in existing models, accept these specific models as the only ones possible (Spicer and Levay, 2012).

In this book, then, the use of Bourdieu's critical view is not a goal in itself but a means of producing new knowledge and a new practice, HOOD, that aims to broaden OD's agenda. HOOD does not attempt to replace OD. On the contrary, it encourages individually oriented OD consultants to keep using therapeutic discourse and practices in order to develop effective helping relationships with consultees. At the same time, HOOD encourages OD consultants to use these specific practices to help consultees develop reflexivity to habitus that generates thoughts and behavior in a way that relates closely to the organization's social structure as well as to the consultees' position in this structure.

HOOD in Other Social Fields

HOOD's focus on habitus and social structure has the potential to help consultants apply effective change and development projects in other fields, such as law and criminology, health and education. Particularly, the concept of habitus can serve consultants with a liberal and democratic approach in these fields by seeing behavior as a result of not only the individual but also the social conditions in which the individual lives and works. In the field of education, for instance, a habitus-oriented approach can help education consultants improve their treatment of unsatisfactory academic success. Putting habitus at the center of the education practice, education consultants would not focus only on improving students' learning skills and other psychological dispositions such as motivation and commitment (Mizrahi, 2009). They would consider as well the students' habitus and use it as a route to the understanding of the social conditions that very often significantly affect low academic achievement: low budgets, lack of education services (such as After School Assistance Programs) and prevailing prejudices toward the community's ethnic groups.

The focus on students' habitus (social dispositions) and on the social conditions from which the habitus develops can also help education consultants to give legitimacy to processes of change. Legitimacy and change processes will grow when consultants stop blaming only the students for academic failure and listen to what students' grades really say in terms of the social context.

Future Research

I have begun a task that demands further conceptual and practical development. Most important is a theoretical development of the intersection of psychological and sociological concepts in framing and coping with organization problems. This meeting point remains unresolved in this book. An investigation of this kind would focus, for instance, on the impact of organizations' structural conditions not only on thoughts and behaviors but also on emotions and other psychological dispositions such as frustration, anxiety and aggression that are also embedded in habitus. The other side of this investigation would search for the role of these specific psychological dispositions in generating organizations' social structures.

A more practical direction, like the one I have started here in chapter seven, would use accepted OD practices, such as guided imagery, role-playing, active listening and group workshops, to develop methodologies for the investigation of consultees' habitus and the social conditions from which this habitus emerges. In general, future practical work of this kind should focus on developing training frameworks to incorporate sociological language, especially the concept of habitus, into the discourse OD consultants use in change processes. This incorporation has a great potential to develop consultants' reflexivity to the subjectivity of consultees in terms not only of self, emotion and other psychological dispositions but also social dispositions, capital and resources, power relations and positions.

Bibliography

Alvesson, M. (1995). *Cultural Perspectives on Organizations*. Cambridge: CUP Archive.
Alvesson, M. (2002). *Understanding Organizational Culture*. Los Angeles, CA: Sage Publications.
Alvesson, M. and H. Willmott (1992). On the idea of emancipation in management and organization studies. *Academy of Management Review*, 17(3), 432–464.
Battilana, J. (2006). Agency and institutions: The enabling role of individuals' social position. *Organization*, 13(5), 653–676.
Beer, M., R. A. Eisenstat and B. Spector (1990). Why change programs don't produce change. *Harvard Business Review*, 68(6), 4–12.
Bourdieu, P. (1977). *Outline of a Theory of Practice*. Cambridge, MA: Cambridge University Press.
Bourdieu, P. (1989). Social space and symbolic power. *Sociological Theory*, 7(1), 14–25.
Bourdieu, P. and L. Wacquant (1992). *An Invitation to Reflexive Sociology*. Chicago, IL and London: University of Chicago Press.
Costea, B., N. Crump and K. Amiridis (2008). Managerialism, the therapeutic habitus and the self in contemporary organizing. *Human Relations*, 61(5), 661–685.
Deetz, S. A. (1992). *Democracy in an Age of Corporate Colonization*. Albany, NY: State University of New York Press.
De Vos, J. (2010). Christopher Lasch's the culture of narcissism: The failure of a critique of psychological politics. *Theory & Psychology*, 20(4), 528–548.
Gergen, K. J. and T. J. Thatchenkery (1996). Developing dialogue for discerning differences. *The Journal of Applied Behavioral Science*, 32(4), 428–433.
Grenfell, M. (2010). Being critical: The practical logic of Bourdieu's metanoia. *Critical Studies in Education*, 51(1), 85–99.
Hackman, J. R. and G. R. Oldham (1976). Motivation through the design of work: Test of a theory. *Organizational Behavior and Human Performance*, 16(2), 250–279.
Hurtado, P. S. (2009). On culture and strategic change: Contrasting the orthodox view with Bourdieu's concept of habitus. *Competition Forum*, 7(1), 205–213.
Illouz, E. (2008). *Saving the Modern Soul: Therapy, Emotions, and the Culture of Self-help*. Berkeley, CA: University of California Press.
Kunda, G. (1992). *Engineering Culture: Control and Commitment in a High-tech Corporation*. Philadelphia, PA: Temple University Press.

Lahire, B. (2002). How to keep a critical tradition alive: A tribute to Pierre Bourdieu. *Review of International Political Economy*, 9(4), 595–600.

Mizrahi, N. (2009). Do not want sociology: Pedagogy without society in the Israeli field of education. (In Hebrew). *Alpayim*, 34, 40–64.

Özbilgin, M., A. Tatli and M. Queen (2005). Book review essay: 'Understanding Bourdieu's contribution to organization and management studies,' [Review of Outline of Theory of Practice; The Logic of Practice; Practical Reason: On the Theory of Action; An Invitation to Reflexive Sociology]. *The Academy of Management Review*, 30(4), 855–869.

Ray, C. A. (1986). Corporate culture: The last frontier of control. *Journal of Management Studies*, 23(3), 287–297.

Schein, E. H. (1969). *Process Consultation: Its Role in Organization Development*. Reading, MA: Addison-Wesley.

Schein, E. H. (1987). *Process Consulting: Lessons for Managers and Consultants.* (Vol. 1). Reading, MA: Addison-Wesley.

Schein, E. H. (2010). *Organizational Culture and Leadership*. San Francisco, CA: Jossey-Bass.

Sewell, Jr., W. H. (1992). A theory of structure: Duality, agency, and transformation. *American Journal of Sociology*, 98(1), 1–29.

Spicer, A. and C. Levay (2012). Critical theories of organizational change. In D. M. Boje, B. Burnes and J. Hassard (Eds.), *The Routledge Companion to Organizational Change*. (pp. 276–290). London and New York: Routledge.

Tatli, A., M. Özbilgin and M. Karatas-Ozkan (2015). Introduction: Management and organization studies meet Pierre Bourdieu. In A. Tatli, M. Özbilgin and M. Karatas-Ozkan (Eds.), *Pierre Bourdieu, Organization, and Management*. London and New York: Routledge.

Voronov, M. and W. P. Woodworth (2012). OD Discourse and Domination. In D. M. Boje, B. Burnes and J. Hassard (Eds.), *The Routledge Companion to Organizational Change*. (pp. 440–455). London and New York: Routledge.

Author Biography

Baruch Shimoni is the founder and head of the Graduate Program in Organization Development at Bar-Ilan University Israel. Shimoni is a professor of sociology and organization development at Bar-Ilan University Israel. He has a Ph.D. from the Hebrew University of Jerusalem. During his Ph.D. studies, he spent a year (1999–2000) at Sloan School of Management at MIT. In the 2003–2005, he had a post-doctoral fellowship at the Department of Anthropology at Yale University. In the course of the last 25 years, he has developed a professional career that integrates academic research with practical consulting to organizations. His challenge has been to both enhance his practical engagement with the most current research and theoretical insights and to use this practical engagement for the development of theory in the OD field. In addition to research and teaching, he founded and now serves as the academic head of the M.A. program in Organization Development and consults with organizations outside the university. In his most recent research project, Professor Shimoni uses the concept of habitus to theoretically and practically understand and cope with processes of change and development. Specifically, he links the Bourdieuan concept of habitus to the field of OD and in so doing provides an alternative way to incorporate the individual and the social in OD.

Index

Note: Page numbers in **bold** indicate tables on the corresponding pages.

Daft, Richard 25
D'Amelio, Angelo 76, **82**
Deetz, Stanley 59
Dent, Eric 74
Dialogic OD (DOD) 27, 29–30;
HOOD *vs* appreciative inquiry and
30–32
Dobbin, Frank 8, 52
doxa: definition 49; field's 48–50

economic capital 4, 44–45
education, HOOD in 119
Eisenstat, Russell 25, 78
entrepreneurship 45
entrepreneurs of small business (ESB) 53
epistemological unconscious 9
Everett, Jeffery 9, 44

field 46; as arenas of competition and
struggle 47–48; as arenas of shared
game 46–47; Bourdieu defining
47; Lewin's concept of 78; Lewin's
theory 22; strategies and doxa of
48–50
Ford, Jeffery 76, **82**
Ford, Laurie 76, **82**
Forson, Cynthia 52
Friedlander, Frank 24

Gergen, Kenneth 28
Goldberg, Susan 74
Goldthorpe, John 6
Greiner, Larry 24
Grenfell, Michael 8

habitus: agent-structure theory and
need for concept of 36–37; concept
of 3–5, 42, 73, 101, 110, 115,
117; economic capital and social
position 44–45; field of OD and
6; interpersonal communication
104; leadership development **105**;
organization culture **105**; power
and influence **106**; search for
103; social change and 100–102;
social context approach 86; social
continuity and 99–100; as source
of thinking and behavior 41–42;
special 42; structure and practice
meeting 37–38
Harvard Business School 12
health, HOOD in 119
Hede, Andrew 74

heresy 49, 50, 51, 52, 53
Herman, S. M., 77
heterodoxy 49, 50
hexis 3
Holocaust 20
Hon, Alice 79
HOOD (habitus-oriented OD) 5–6;
appreciative inquiry and dialogic
OD *vs* 30–32; bridge between
organizations and society 65,
110–111; case study of surgery
department 93, 94–96; dual
perspective of 7–8; empowerment,
emancipation and social structure
111–113; habitus and social change
100–102; habitus and social
continuity 99–100; as helping
profession 6–7; interpersonal
communication **104**; leadership
development **105**; objectives
102–104; objectives of OD and
102; in OD practices 104–106;
organization culture **105**; in other
social fields 119; power and
influence **106**; problem solving
and change 96–98; psychological
dispositions 32; resistance to change
(RTC) and **82**, 85–89; skills for
operating in accordance with 113;
social dispositions 46, **82**, 85, 94,
97, 102, **102**, 109, 119; source of
thinking and behavior **21**
Huault, Isabelle 66
human capital 4, 44
humanistic values, organization
development (OD) 61
hysteresis 43–44

Illouz, Eva 57, 59
individualism 41; blame and control
57–58; position of authority 58
individualistic orientation:
psychologists' era of OD (1960s)
23–25; source of thinking and
behavior **21**
institutional entrepreneurship 45
interpersonal communication, OD
practices **104**

Jaffe, Cynthia 74
Jefferson, Andrew 41
Jenkins, Richard 50
Jermier, John 74

Thompson, James 6
toys of social forces 9
training group (T-group):
  individualistic orientation 24;
  Lewin 22–23; self-development and
  growth 32; sensitivity **21**, 22, 61

Vandenberghe, Frederic 99, 100
Van de Ven, Andrew 10

Vaughan, Diane 41
Voronov, Maxim 10, 62

Waclawski, Janine 61
Waddell, Dianne 76
Weick, Karl 25
Whatley, Art 10
Willmott, Hugh 66
Woodworth, Warner 62